CONTENTS

THE SCIENCE OF HAPPINESS

Lessons From Positive Psychology

Dr Bhaskar Bora

A PERSONAL NOTE FROM THE AUTHOR

My journey, once marked by certainty and driven by purpose, has transformed in ways I could never have anticipated. It is no longer about grand achievements or the pursuit of external success, but about the quiet, tender moments that reveal the true essence of life—moments of love, care, and presence. What you hold in your hands is not just a collection of words, but a testament to resilience, a story woven from the delicate threads of struggle, acceptance, and ultimately, renewal.

There was a time when my life flowed with the grace of a symphony, every note in perfect harmony. As a doctor, my days were filled with the pulse of life itself—offering hope, easing suffering, and healing with steady hands. The white coat I wore wasn't just a symbol of my profession; it embodied my very identity; an outward reflection of the healer I believed I was destined to be. The lives I touched, the people I helped—it all gave profound meaning to my existence.

But life, in its mysterious and unpredictable ways, had other plans. In one swift, unforeseen moment, the world I knew unravelled. First came the spinal cord injury, stripping away the physical strength I had relied upon. Then, the shadow of cancer darkened the horizon, a stark reminder of life's fragility. The world of medicine, where I once found so much joy and purpose, suddenly slipped away, leaving a vast emptiness in its wake—a silence where once there had been meaning.

Gone were the bustling corridors of the hospital, replaced by the quiet solitude of my home. No longer a "Doctor," I found myself standing at the edge of an uncertain future, my hands—once so steady with the knowledge of healing—trembling with questions I wasn't ready to face. Without the title, without the work that had defined me for so long, who was I? What was left of me when everything I had known was no longer within reach?

In that silence, in the stillness of a life interrupted, I began to uncover something unexpected. The role of a disabled husband and father, once a distant concept, became my new reality—one that held unexpected grace. What began as an effort to nurture my relationships, to find solace in this new world, slowly evolved into a profound inward journey.

I found healing in the spiritual—a rhythm of meditation, reading, and reflection that allowed me to rediscover the parts of myself I thought were lost. As I immersed myself in books, audiobooks, and hours of research, I began to understand that this new chapter of my life was not an ending, but a rebirth. The solitude of these years, the quiet hours of writing and reflection, gave birth to the very pages you hold in your hands now.

It is with deep gratitude that I share these words with you, knowing that they carry with them not just knowledge, but a piece of my soul. I hope that these reflections and insights offer you a fresh perspective on life and perhaps some nourishment for your own journey.

We cannot control what the universe throws at us, but how we react to those curveballs defines who we are and what we make of our lives.

INTRODUCTION: A JOURNEY TOWARD JOY

There is a moment—small and delicate—that lives within each of us, like a soft whisper on a windy day. It is the fleeting memory of laughter shared beneath the open sky, the faint aroma of childhood breakfasts, the quiet peace that accompanies the end of a good day. It is here, in these subtle remnants of joy, that the seeds of happiness are sown, waiting patiently to grow, to bloom, to remind us of life's sweetest truths.

Happiness is often described as elusive, a fragile spark that slips through our fingers the moment we recognize it. But what if happiness is less a destination and more a state of being, woven into the fabric of our lives, threaded through each experience, each choice, and each breath? What if joy does not need to be chased or captured but simply noticed, honoured, nurtured?

This book is a humble attempt to decode that mysterious feeling, that ineffable glow we call happiness. Through the lens of positive psychology, I invite you to journey into the depths of human experience, where science and spirit intermingle, where neurons spark and hearts awaken. Here, happiness is not reduced to mere optimism or a cheerful temperament; it is a mosaic—a kaleidoscope of moments, habits, and intentions that shape our lives in ways we seldom recognize.

In recent years, the study of happiness has transformed, moving from the realm of mystics and poets to the laboratories of scientists and psychologists. The new science of happiness has uncovered truths that echo what ancient wisdom has long told us: that joy is both an art and a practice, requiring not only our attention but also our intention. Positive psychology, a field dedicated to understanding and enhancing human well-being, offers profound insights into how we can cultivate a life rich in meaning, purpose, and authentic joy.

This journey will lead us through some of life's most precious landscapes: resilience, gratitude, kindness, love, and purpose. Each chapter will open a door into a different realm of joy, exploring the ways our minds, our actions, and our connections shape the happiness we experience. The path is both scientific and soulful, blending research with reflection, knowledge with wonder.

As we embark on this exploration, let us hold one simple truth close: happiness is not perfection. It is not the absence of sorrow or a life devoid of challenges. It is, instead, the art of finding light in the midst of shadows, of embracing each moment as it comes, and of savouring the beauty of what it means to be truly alive.

Throughout these pages, I encourage you to journey slowly, to pause and ponder, to allow the ideas to settle gently, like seeds on fertile ground. This book is not a formula; it is a companion. May each chapter bring you closer to the joy that resides within, a joy as unique and timeless as the stars above.

Welcome, dear reader, to the science of happiness. May it inspire you not only to seek happiness but to create it, to live it, to become it.

CHAPTER 1: PRELUDE TO HAPPINESS – THE QUEST FOR FULFILMENT

Happiness. Such a simple word, yet within its five letters resides a boundless universe—a universe filled with dreams, yearnings, and the heartbeat of life itself. Across cultures and epochs, through the rise and fall of civilizations, happiness has been the quiet flame that fuels human endeavour. It is the whisper that calls to each of us in the dark hours, a beacon guiding us forward, and the invisible thread that binds us in our shared humanity.

What is it that we seek in happiness? Is it a flash of ecstasy, fleeting and ephemeral, or a deep wellspring, steadfast and eternal? To understand happiness is to embrace the paradox of longing: to want without possessing, to journey without arriving, to revel in the search as much as the discovery. Here lies the essence of happiness—not as a destination to be reached but as a way of walking through the world, with eyes open to the radiance in the mundane, the miracle in the minuscule.

From ancient sages to modern scientists, from monks in meditation to poets in contemplation, humans have endeavoured to grasp the elusive nature of happiness. The Greeks, with their unrelenting thirst for wisdom, called it eudaimonia—a life of flourishing and virtue. In their eyes, happiness was less an emotional state and more a condition of the soul, achieved through balance, purpose, and the cultivation of one's highest self. The ancient sages of India spoke of ananda, the bliss that rises from union with the divine, a joy untouched by life's ebb and flow. And today, in the laboratories of positive psychology, we see happiness not merely as pleasure but as well-being—a tapestry woven of purpose, resilience, and connection.

Yet even with all these descriptions, happiness remains indefinable. Perhaps this is the secret of its allure. Happiness, by nature, resists our attempts to cage it in words or measurements. It is a feeling, an experience, a state that transcends reason. To grasp happiness, we must look not only outward but inward. We must learn to listen to the quiet stirrings of our own hearts, to see the beauty in simplicity, and to appreciate the grace that dwells in moments of stillness.

The Call of the Human Spirit

There exists in each of us a yearning, a quiet but persistent call—a call for something more, something beyond the confines of daily routines and fleeting pleasures. It is a longing as old as time itself, a thirst for meaning, for depth, for connection. This call is the first whisper of happiness, a reminder that life holds more than survival, more than mere existence. It invites us to seek fulfilment not in what we acquire but in what we become.

The path to happiness is, at its core, a path of self-discovery. It is a journey into the recesses of the heart, a quest to unearth our deepest desires, our truest aspirations. As we peel back the layers of societal expectations, we begin to touch the authentic self—a self unburdened by comparisons, free from the need to impress, complete in its quiet dignity.

To heed this call is to step into the world with wonder, to view life not as a series of demands but as a gift to be unwrapped, slowly and with reverence. When we see the world through this lens, we realize that happiness does not reside in some distant future or in the possession of perfect circumstances. Rather, it exists here and now, waiting to be uncovered in the details, in the delicate, ephemeral moments that make up a life.

The Subtle Art of Contentment

In a world driven by the pursuit of "more"—more success, wealth, recognition—contentment is a radical act. It is a gentle rebellion against society's ceaseless clamour, a quiet insistence that there is beauty in enough. Contentment does not ask us to abandon our dreams or to settle for less; rather, it invites us to cherish what we have, to find joy in the here and now, to embrace the richness of each moment.

Imagine a life where the small becomes sacred—a sip

of morning tea, a shared smile, a walk in the evening light. Happiness is found not in the grandiose but in the simple pleasures, those precious instants that slip by almost unnoticed, like petals falling in the breeze. In these moments of contentment, we touch a deeper joy, a joy that is less about exhilaration and more about peace—a joy that whispers, "All is well. You are where you are meant to be."

To cultivate contentment is to make a choice: to choose presence over distraction, gratitude over yearning, and simplicity over complexity. It is to recognize that life's gifts are often subtle and require our quiet attention. As we learn to slow down and savour, we find that happiness is not a product of circumstances but a state of mind, a deliberate way of being.

The Journey, Not the Destination

If there is one lesson that happiness teaches us, it is that life is a journey. Each step, each breath, each experience is part of an unfolding story—a story written not in achievements but in moments of connection, of laughter, of grace. The journey toward happiness is one of becoming, of continuous transformation, of embracing each chapter of life with open arms and an open heart.

In this way, happiness is not a finish line; it is a compass. It points us toward those things that nourish our souls, that enliven our spirits, that give meaning to our days. Happiness asks us to live not in expectation of some future moment but in the fullness of now, to walk with curiosity and compassion, to see the world as a landscape rich with wonder.

The wise have long told us that happiness is found within, and yet, how often we look outward, believing that joy can be attained through possessions or status. But the true path to fulfilment requires us to turn inward, to cultivate qualities of mind and heart that remain untouched by the winds of circumstance. It is in the soil of kindness, of generosity, of acceptance that happiness takes root and flourishes.

The Subtle Wonders of Existence

Perhaps, at its core, happiness is an invitation to marvel, to behold the world with the eyes of a child, to see every sunrise as a miracle, every leaf as a masterpiece. It is to breathe in the fullness of life, to cherish the marvel that we are here, alive, capable of wonder and joy. In the end, happiness is less about what we do and more about how we see. It is a way of looking at life, of recognizing the extraordinary in the ordinary, of finding beauty in the unremarkable.

As we embark on this journey, let us do so with open hearts, with a willingness to see beyond the surface, to discover the treasures that lie hidden in plain sight. For happiness, like life itself, is a gift—a gift that asks us not to seek but to savour, not to possess but to appreciate. May we, in this exploration, find not only the science of happiness but the art of truly living.

Happiness as a Quiet Awakening

Imagine for a moment that happiness is a dawn—a gradual light spreading across the sky, gentle yet profound. It begins as the faintest glimmer, an almost imperceptible hue that brushes the horizon, unnoticed by those who rush through the hours. But for those who pause, who allow themselves the luxury of stillness, happiness becomes a quiet awakening, a recognition that life itself is a series of small miracles unfolding before our very eyes.

In these tranquil spaces, where the heart rests easy and the mind quiets, we catch glimpses of something timeless and tender. Happiness is not loud; it is a whisper, a murmur that beckons us to listen, to attune ourselves to the present moment. And yet, how often do we seek it in the clamour, believing that joy can be seized through action, through acquisition? We search for happiness as if it were a prize, a trophy, something to be won and held high. But happiness resists such capture. It asks not to be grasped but to be noticed, to be welcomed like the first light of day.

To awaken to happiness is to awaken to ourselves—to the breath within our lungs, the warmth of our own skin, the rhythm of our heartbeat. It is to realize that joy resides not in some distant goal but in the aliveness we carry within, in the unfolding wonder of our own existence.

The Unseen Shores of Joy

Life often feels like a journey across uncharted seas, our souls drifting toward unseen shores. We chase one horizon after another, hoping that perhaps the next wave will bring us to the land of our dreams. But happiness, it seems, lies not on the distant shore but in the journey itself—in the breeze that fills our sails, the stars that guide us, the water lapping gently at the edges of our vessel. Happiness is in the drift, in the dance, in the unhurried unfolding of each moment.

Yet, in our endless quest for "more," how many of us miss the treasures that already surround us? The touch of a loved one's hand, the laughter shared in dimly lit rooms, the smell of earth after rain—these are the true gems, the pearls scattered along our path, waiting to be noticed. In the pursuit of distant goals, we often forget the riches within arm's reach, overlooking the beauty that life so generously offers.

What if we were to look upon each day as a blessing, each interaction as an opportunity for connection, each breath as a reminder of our aliveness? Happiness, then, is not an end but an ethos—a way of moving through the world with gratitude, with wonder, with a sense of reverence for all that is. It is a choice to dwell in appreciation, to see beauty in the transient, to love what is fleeting, knowing that it too is part of the great, intricate dance of existence.

Echoes from Ancient Wisdom

The ancients, in their wisdom, understood this truth well. The philosophers of Greece, the mystics of India, the sages of China—they all spoke of happiness not as pleasure, but as a deeper, more abiding state. They taught that true joy is found in balance, in harmony, in the alignment of our lives with the rhythms of nature and spirit. For them, happiness was not something to be added to life but a way of being—a choice to live in accordance with one's highest values, to cultivate inner richness rather than outward wealth.

Aristotle, the great philosopher, called it eudaimonia— the flourishing of the human spirit. He saw happiness not as mere gratification but as a state achieved through virtue, through the exercise of wisdom, courage, and kindness. To live well, he believed, was to live with purpose, to align one's actions with one's values, to strive for the good not only for oneself but for all.

So too did the Buddha, who spoke of the inner peace that arises when one transcends desire, when one lets go of attachment and embraces compassion. In his teachings, happiness is the natural state of a mind unburdened by craving, a heart that dwells in loving-kindness. For him, happiness was the stillness at the centre of the storm, the clarity that comes when one sees life as it truly is—impermanent, interconnected, sacred.

And yet, while these ancient voices call to us from across the ages, how often do we heed their wisdom? How often do we pause to consider what it means to truly live well, to cultivate happiness not as a fleeting feeling but as a way of being?

The Alchemy of Gratitude

Gratitude. It is the quiet alchemy that turns what we have into enough, that transforms the ordinary into the extraordinary. In the light of gratitude, every experience, no matter how small, becomes precious; every encounter, no matter how brief, becomes meaningful. Gratitude is the lens through which happiness is magnified, the doorway through which contentment enters.

Imagine the life that could be lived if gratitude were its foundation. Each day would become a prayer, each moment a sacred offering. The smallest acts—a stranger's smile, a bird's song, the warmth of the sun on our skin

—would be met with wonder, with appreciation, with the knowledge that we are blessed beyond measure. In gratitude, we find happiness not as a possession but as a perspective, a way of looking at the world that transforms scarcity into abundance, expectation into acceptance.

Gratitude invites us to see life as a gift, to treat each day as a rare and wondrous opportunity. And in this shift, we find a happiness that is not fragile but resilient, a joy that does not wane in the face of hardship but grows richer with time.

Living in the Present: The Art of Presence

The present moment. It is all we ever truly have, yet it is often the most neglected. In our haste to reach the future, we leave the present behind, treating it as a mere stepping stone to something greater, something more. But what if the present is the only place where happiness can truly exist? What if joy is not found in the anticipation of what might be, but in the full embrace of what is?

To live in the present is to dance with life itself, to flow with its rhythms, to savour each instant as it comes. It is to realize that happiness cannot be postponed, cannot be placed on hold until circumstances align. Happiness exists only in the now, in this breath, in this heartbeat, in this fleeting, fragile moment.

Living in the present is an art, a discipline, a practice that asks us to let go of regret and fear, to release the burden of past and future, and to open ourselves to the fullness of each experience. It is a call to be awake, to be mindful, to be fully alive.

The Quest Continues

And so, dear reader, the quest for happiness unfolds not in grand revelations but in gentle awakenings. It is a path that asks us to travel light, to carry with us only what serves, to let go of what no longer nourishes. Happiness, it turns out, is not about gathering but about shedding, not about seeking but about seeing. It is a journey inward, a pilgrimage of the soul, a return to the heart's deepest knowing.

As you walk this path, may you do so with a spirit of wonder, with eyes attuned to the beauty of the world around you, with a heart open to the blessings that each day brings. Happiness, after all, is less a place to arrive at than a way of moving through the world. It is found not in the grand achievements but in the quiet moments, the sacred spaces, the tender whispers of a life well-lived.

In the chapters that follow, we will journey deeper into this landscape, exploring the science and soul of happiness, unlocking the secrets that lie within and around us. But for now, let us pause here, in this moment, in this beginning. Let us recognize that happiness is already here, waiting, like an old friend, like a familiar song, ready to guide us home.

CHAPTER 2: THE ANATOMY OF JOY – UNDERSTANDING POSITIVE EMOTIONS

Happiness, that ephemeral sensation that lifts our spirits and colours our days, is not merely a feeling; it is a symphony within, a delicate orchestration of mind and body. Beneath each smile, each laugh, each moment of contentment lies a symphony of chemistry, an interplay of tiny, invisible forces working in harmony to create the sensation of joy. Like unseen architects, these molecules and hormones build the foundations of bliss, shaping our moods, lifting our spirits, and guiding our hearts toward joy.

In this chapter, we dive into the mysterious alchemy that is happiness, exploring the quiet, unseen forces that move within us, that lift our spirits, and paint our experiences with the colours of joy. Through endorphins, dopamine, serotonin, and oxytocin, the body reveals itself to be a master of its own happiness, an artist crafting emotions with unparalleled precision. To understand this inner world is to catch a glimpse of the beauty within—a beauty as intricate as it is profound.

The Symphony Begins: The Role of Endorphins

Imagine, for a moment, that joy is a melody—a gentle tune played within us, soft and harmonious. The first notes of this melody are often struck by endorphins, those quiet chemists of comfort, who rush in when we need relief from pain, from sadness, from the heaviness of life. Endorphins are the body's natural balm, a soothing whisper that tells us, "It will be all right."

These tiny molecules, released during laughter, exercise, or even the simple act of eating, serve as nature's analgesics, easing both physical and emotional pain. They flood our bodies when we move, when we breathe deeply, when we immerse ourselves in activities that bring us alive. In those moments when we are lost in the beauty of movement, be it a dance, a jog, or a simple stretch, endorphins work quietly, easing the edges of our discomfort and reminding us of the peace within.

But endorphins do more than numb pain; they invite us into joy. They are the first brushstrokes on the canvas of happiness, setting the stage for deeper, more complex emotions. With each release, they gently lift our spirits, making room for the more vibrant hues of bliss. Endorphins teach us that happiness is not merely the absence of pain, but a presence—a calm, enduring comfort that makes room for beauty, for pleasure, for life's tender moments.

The Thrill of Discovery: Dopamine and the Pursuit of Joy

As the symphony of happiness builds, dopamine enters, bringing with it the thrill of anticipation, the joy of discovery, the spark of motivation. Dopamine is the molecule of desire, the chemical of curiosity, the architect of dreams. It is the force that propels us forward, that ignites our passions, that makes us reach for more, for better, for the new and unknown.

Imagine the rush of dopamine as a spark that lights up the brain, illuminating paths of possibility and purpose. It flows in moments of excitement, in the pursuit of a goal, in the thrill of an idea taking shape. When we set our sights on something—a new project, a skill, a journey —it is dopamine that fuels our persistence, our drive, our hunger for achievement. It gives us energy to pursue, to strive, to awaken to the infinite potentials within and around us.

Dopamine invites us to dream, to envision a life richer, fuller, more alive. It encourages us to move, to explore, to transform our inner aspirations into outward reality. And in each step, each small victory, it rewards us with that unmistakable surge of joy, reminding us that the journey itself is a source of happiness, a path lined with moments of quiet elation.

But dopamine is also a teacher, reminding us that happiness is not merely found in the end result, but in the pursuit, in the exploration, in the dance of becoming. It whispers to us that joy is woven into the very act of reaching, that in each step toward fulfilment lies the essence of happiness.

The Balm of Contentment: Serotonin and the Peace Within

As dopamine fades, making way for quieter emotions, serotonin takes its place—a gentle tide that washes over us, filling us with calm, with satisfaction, with a sense of belonging. Serotonin is the molecule of contentment, the architect of inner peace, the whisper that says, "You are enough, and this moment is enough."

Where dopamine brings excitement, serotonin offers solace. It flows when we feel safe, when we feel loved, when we feel connected to something greater than ourselves. Released through acts of kindness, through the warmth of the sun, through moments of mindfulness, serotonin reminds us that joy is not merely found in doing, but in being. It is the feeling of lying in the grass, of watching the clouds drift by, of knowing that we are part of a larger, beautiful whole.

Serotonin teaches us that happiness does not always demand action, that joy can be found in stillness, in solitude, in the quiet embrace of the present moment. It is the warmth in a hug, the peace in a silent gaze, the tranquillity of simply existing without striving. Through serotonin, we learn that happiness is not only the thrill of life but also its serenity, its grace, its gentle acceptance of what is.

The Bond of Belonging: Oxytocin and the Joy of Connection

Finally, there is oxytocin, the molecule of love, the guardian of trust, the silent weaver of bonds that make us human. Oxytocin is the force that binds, that connects, that opens our hearts to one another. It is released in moments of affection, in gestures of compassion, in the shared laughter of friends, in the tender touch of a loved one.

Oxytocin teaches us that happiness is not a solitary pursuit but a shared experience, a dance of connection that weaves us into the fabric of each other's lives. It is in our relationships, in our friendships, in our communities that we find the deepest joys, the most profound fulfilment. Oxytocin reminds us that we are not alone, that we are held, cherished, seen.

Through the release of oxytocin, we come to understand the power of belonging, of being part of something larger than ourselves. It is the happiness of shared memories, of quiet companionship, of love given and received without condition. Oxytocin invites us to open our hearts, to let others in, to find happiness in the spaces between us.

A Delicate Harmony: The Dance of Emotions

In the dance of endorphins, dopamine, serotonin, and oxytocin, we find a symphony of joy, a delicate harmony that lifts us, comforts us, propels us, connects us. Each molecule plays its part, creating a tapestry of emotions that shapes our lives in ways we often take for granted. Together, they teach us that happiness is not a single emotion but a rich, complex experience woven from many threads, each one adding its own colour to the canvas of our lives.

This chemical symphony is a reminder of the miracle within, of the incredible capacity of the human body to create joy, to heal, to connect, to thrive. It shows us that happiness is not something to be found outside ourselves but something that is generated, nurtured, and sustained within. With every breath, every heartbeat, every moment of awareness, we are given the tools to cultivate our own happiness, to build a life of meaning, of purpose, of joy.

As we continue this journey, let us do so with a sense of wonder for the beauty within us, for the hidden forces that guide us toward happiness, for the quiet magic of biology and psychology that shapes our lives. In understanding the anatomy of joy, we come to see that happiness is not an accident but a choice, a craft, an art that we create each day. And as we nurture this symphony within, may we find a happiness that is both vibrant and enduring, both individual and shared—a happiness that reflects the infinite beauty of the human soul.

CHAPTER 3: THE ALCHEMY OF THE MIND – POWER OF THOUGHTS IN HAPPINESS

The mind is a vast landscape, an intricate garden where seeds of thought take root, growing into the flowers and fruits of our experience. Within this inner world, our thoughts are like invisible hands, sculpting the contours of our reality, painting our days with hues of joy or shadow, weaving the fabric of what we call happiness. To understand the alchemy of the mind is to uncover a profound truth: that happiness is often less about what happens to us and more about how we perceive it, how we choose to see and respond to the events that life unfolds.

In this chapter, we step into the sacred realm of thoughts, exploring the transformative power they hold, the ways they shape not only our emotions but our very sense of self. Through the practices of positivity, resilience, and mindfulness, we are invited to become alchemists of our own minds, to learn the art of turning ordinary thoughts into tools for cultivating joy and inner peace. For in the alchemy of the mind lies the secret to a happiness that endures—a happiness that rises not from circumstance, but from a heart and mind trained to see beauty, grace, and possibility.

The Lens of Perception: Shaping Reality with Thoughts

Imagine, if you will, that each thought is a lens through which we view the world—a filter that colours our perceptions, that frames what we see, that defines how we feel. A thought, though fleeting, has the power to transform a moment, to cast it in light or shadow, to make it a source of joy or sorrow. And while we often believe our thoughts are mere responses to reality, the truth is that they are creators of reality, shaping our experience from the inside out.

When we choose thoughts that lift us, that inspire us, that bring clarity and understanding, we create a world bathed in light, a reality filled with possibilities. But when we dwell on thoughts of doubt, fear, or resentment, we create walls that block the light, imprisoning us in shadows of our own making. This is the alchemy of the mind: the power to transform any experience through the lens of perception, to choose thoughts that uplift rather than diminish, to see each moment as an opportunity for growth, for love, for happiness.

Through this lens, even hardship becomes a teacher, even loss a doorway to greater wisdom. The mind becomes not a battleground but a sanctuary, a place where we can retreat, reflect, and renew our spirits. In choosing our thoughts, we choose our world; in shaping our perceptions, we shape our lives.

The Gold of Positivity: Cultivating Joy in Each Moment

Positivity is the first ingredient in the alchemy of happiness. It is the art of seeing beauty in the everyday, of finding silver linings in life's clouds, of allowing even the smallest pleasures to fill us with joy. Positivity does not deny the presence of hardship or sorrow; rather, it chooses to see beyond them, to hold on to the light even when surrounded by darkness.

When we cultivate positivity, we become like artists, painting our lives with colours of hope, gratitude, and wonder. Each moment becomes an opportunity to find something beautiful, to celebrate the simple, to cherish what is often overlooked. Positivity is not a denial of reality but a choice to embrace it with grace, to find joy not only in life's highs but in its lows, in its quiet corners, in its ordinary days.

Through positivity, we learn to see happiness not as a distant peak but as a journey, a series of small steps taken with a grateful heart. We realize that happiness is not about waiting for the perfect moment but creating it, nurturing it, allowing it to blossom in the spaces between our dreams and our realities. In choosing positivity, we choose to live fully, to open ourselves to the beauty that each day offers, to celebrate the miracle of simply being.

The Strength of Resilience: Rising with Grace

If positivity is the art of seeing the light, resilience is the art of withstanding the storm. It is the strength that allows us to bend without breaking, to rise after every fall, to find joy not only in triumph but in the courage to try again. Resilience is the alchemy of turning hardship into wisdom, of transforming setbacks into stepping stones, of choosing not to be defined by our struggles but to be refined by them.

Resilience is born not from avoiding pain but from embracing it, from facing life's challenges with an open heart, from trusting that within each difficulty lies the seed of growth. It is the quiet confidence that we are capable of enduring, of thriving, of finding beauty even in the scars that life leaves behind. Resilience teaches us that happiness is not a fragile thing, easily shattered by adversity, but a deep, abiding strength, a light that shines brightest in the darkest of times.

To cultivate resilience is to cultivate hope, to remind ourselves that no storm lasts forever, that within us lies a wellspring of strength, a capacity for joy that cannot be extinguished. Through resilience, we find a happiness that is steadfast, that endures, that grows stronger with each challenge we face. In resilience, we discover a joy that is rooted not in circumstance but in the unwavering belief in our own ability to heal, to learn, to rise.

The Art of Mindfulness: Embracing the Present

Mindfulness is perhaps the most profound practice in the alchemy of happiness. It is the art of being fully present, of immersing ourselves in the now, of letting go of past regrets and future anxieties to embrace the richness of this very moment. Mindfulness is the doorway to inner peace, a path to a happiness that is as simple as a breath, as steady as a heartbeat, as constant as the present moment.

To be mindful is to savour life in its smallest details—the taste of a sip of tea, the warmth of sunlight on the skin, the sound of a loved one's voice. It is to recognize that happiness is not found in the grand or the distant but in the quiet, the everyday, the fleeting. In mindfulness, we learn to slow down, to listen, to see with new eyes, to appreciate the miracle of simply being alive.

Through mindfulness, we come to understand that the mind is not a prison but a garden, a place where we can plant seeds of peace, of joy, of compassion. We learn that happiness is not about accumulating more but about appreciating what already is, about finding contentment in the here and now. Mindfulness invites us to let go of the need for constant change, to be at peace with the moment, to find beauty in what is.

The Alchemy of Choice: Crafting a Life of Joy

Ultimately, the power of the mind lies in choice. We choose the thoughts we hold, the beliefs we cultivate, the perceptions we entertain. Each choice is a stroke on the canvas of our lives, a step in the dance of our days. In choosing positivity, we create a world filled with light; in choosing resilience, we build a strength that carries us through; in choosing mindfulness, we find peace in the present.

This is the alchemy of the mind—a gentle, powerful transformation that invites us to see the world not as it is but as it can be. It is the art of crafting happiness from within, of creating joy not from what we have but from how we see, how we feel, how we choose to live. In this alchemy, we find a happiness that is steady, profound, unshakable—a happiness that is not bound by circumstances but shaped by the heart.

As we continue this journey, let us remember that happiness is within our reach, waiting to be cultivated, nurtured, embraced. May we become alchemists of our own minds, turning our thoughts into tools for joy, our perceptions into pathways to peace, our lives into testaments of the beauty of the human spirit.

Happiness is not a destination but a way of seeing, a way of being, a way of living with open eyes, an open mind, and an open heart.

CHAPTER 4: ENCHANTMENT IN THE EVERYDAY – FINDING BEAUTY IN THE MUNDANE

In a world that often glorifies the extraordinary, the grand, the exceptional, there exists a quiet magic in the everyday moments we so easily overlook. The enchantment of the mundane lies not in spectacle but in subtlety—a gentle reminder that happiness need not be sought in the rare or distant. It can be found, softly nestled, in the warmth of morning light streaming through a window, in the laughter shared over a simple meal, in the rhythmic sound of rain against the roof. The ordinary moments, the ones we pass by in our haste, hold within them a secret charm, a quiet beauty that whispers to us, calling us to pause, to notice, to cherish.

In this chapter, we delve into the art of presence, into the practice of mindfulness that allows us to uncover the beauty hidden in the simplest of moments. For when we learn to see the enchantment in the everyday, life itself becomes a gift, a series of treasures waiting to be discovered. The mundane transforms into the marvellous, and we come to understand that happiness is not a distant peak to be reached but a gentle grace woven into each passing moment.

The Quiet Magic of Mornings

There is a hushed, sacred quality to mornings, an innocence that belongs only to the beginning of the day. Before the world awakens fully, before the noise and rush begin, there exists a moment of pure possibility— a moment in which the day lies open before us, waiting to be filled. In these early hours, we are gifted a pause, a quietness that invites us to breathe deeply, to savour, to feel gratitude for the simple act of waking.

Imagine waking slowly, feeling the coolness of sheets, the warmth of sunlight tracing patterns across the wall. There is no rush here, no urgency—only the calm invitation to step gently into the day. Perhaps there is a cup of tea waiting, steam rising in delicate tendrils, a warmth that cradles the hands and stirs the soul. These moments, small and unassuming, are imbued with a gentle beauty, a reminder that life's loveliness does not demand grandeur.

When we approach each morning with this reverence, with this appreciation for the softness of beginnings, we set the tone for the day. We carry with us a sense of wonder, a readiness to see the beauty in all that follows. And in doing so, we create a happiness that is not dependent on what the day will bring but on our own willingness to see the enchantment in its unfolding.

Finding Poetry in the Routine

There is a certain poetry in the routines we perform, the familiar rhythms that shape our days. These acts —washing dishes, folding laundry, preparing meals— might seem mundane, yet within them lies a hidden grace. When we move through these tasks with mindfulness, with presence, we transform them into rituals, into small acts of devotion that connect us to the fabric of life itself.

Consider the simple act of preparing a meal. There is beauty in the act of chopping vegetables, in the sound of water boiling, in the aroma that fills the room as ingredients blend together. Each step, each movement, is an invitation to slow down, to be fully present, to engage with the senses. And as we immerse ourselves in these everyday acts, we find that they offer a quiet satisfaction, a joy that comes not from what we accomplish but from how we approach it.

In this way, routines become moments of mindfulness, opportunities to practice presence, to bring awareness to the here and now. We find poetry in the ordinary, a rhythm in the repetitive, a melody in the mundane. And through this awareness, we cultivate a happiness that is rooted not in novelty but in appreciation, in a deep, abiding love for the simplicity of life.

The Beauty of Small Moments

Happiness is often thought of as something grand, something that arrives in bursts of excitement or achievement. But true happiness, the kind that sustains, is woven from the small moments—the fleeting, often unnoticed instants that make up our days. It is the beauty of a single leaf, traced in veins of green and gold, or the sparkle of sunlight on water, or the quiet of a night filled with stars.

To see the beauty in these small moments is to cultivate an open heart, a mind attuned to wonder. It is to approach life with the curiosity of a child, with eyes that see not only what is but what could be, with a spirit willing to be moved by the simple and the subtle. For when we learn to see the beauty in a single moment, we come to understand that happiness is not a rare event but a state of awareness, a way of seeing the world that is available to us in each breath, in each heartbeat.

This is the gift of presence, the treasure of mindfulness—a happiness that is not found in things or achievements but in our own capacity to notice, to savour, to be fully here.

Mindfulness as an Invitation to Enchantment

Mindfulness is often described as the art of being present, of bringing one's full awareness to the moment at hand. But it is more than that—it is an invitation to enchantment, a call to see the world as an endless tapestry of wonder, woven from moments that are both fleeting and eternal.

When we practice mindfulness, we become like explorers in our own lives, discovering beauty in the most unexpected places. The texture of a blanket, the taste of a piece of fruit, the sound of wind in the trees—all become sources of joy, reminders of the richness that surrounds us. Mindfulness asks us to slow down, to pay attention, to allow ourselves to be captivated by the world as it is, without longing for more or wishing for different.

In this way, mindfulness transforms the ordinary into the extraordinary. It invites us to see life not as a series of tasks to be completed but as a collection of experiences to be cherished. Each moment becomes a gift, a source of happiness that is not dependent on what we have or what we achieve but on our willingness to be present, to be open, to be alive.

The Art of Savouring

To savour is to linger, to extend the life of a moment by immersing ourselves fully in it. It is the act of drawing out joy, of holding happiness in our hands a little longer, of allowing it to fill us completely. Savouring is a practice, an art, a skill that invites us to deepen our experience of life, to taste its richness, to appreciate its texture.

Imagine savouring a moment as one would savour a piece of chocolate, letting it melt slowly, enjoying each nuance of flavour, each hint of sweetness. To savour is to give ourselves fully to an experience, to let it fill us, to let it leave an imprint on our hearts. It is the opposite of rushing, of skimming through life. Savouring is the antidote to hurry, a way of slowing down, of finding pleasure in each moment, of celebrating the here and now.

Through savouring, we find that happiness need not be loud or intense. It can be gentle, quiet, a simple contentment that lingers, that deepens, that grows richer with each passing moment. In savouring, we discover a happiness that is as steady as it is profound, a joy that resides not in the future but in the present, in the moments we choose to hold close.

An Invitation to See Differently

As we walk through life, may we learn to see with new eyes, to approach each day as an opportunity to uncover beauty in the unexpected, in the overlooked, in the mundane. May we cultivate a sense of wonder, a spirit of appreciation, a love for the small miracles that fill our days. For in the enchantment of the everyday, we find a happiness that is steady, that is true, that is woven into the fabric of life itself.

Let us find joy in the act of living, in the simple pleasure of breathing, of being, of belonging to this world. Let us learn to cherish the ordinary, to see the marvel in the mundane, to understand that happiness is not something we must chase but something we can find, here and now, in the enchantment of each passing moment.

For when we learn to see the world in this way, happiness is no longer something outside of us, something we must seek or capture. It becomes a part of who we are, a way of moving through life with grace, with gratitude, with a heart open to the beauty in all things.

CHAPTER 5: THE VIRTUE OF GRATITUDE – A PORTAL TO CONTENTMENT

There is a quiet, unassuming power in gratitude—a force as gentle as a sigh, yet as profound as a sunrise breaking over a darkened horizon. Gratitude is the art of seeing life through a lens of appreciation, of holding even the smallest blessings in reverence. It is a way of saying "thank you" not only for what we have but for what we are, for the beauty that surrounds us, and for the love we share. Gratitude is the alchemy that transforms our ordinary days into precious memories, our simple moments into sacred ones, our lives into something rich and meaningful.

Gratitude asks for nothing in return; it is a gift we give freely, both to others and to ourselves. And in this giving, we find a happiness that is gentle, steady, enduring—a happiness that does not rely on possessions or accomplishments but on a heart that is open, that is humble, that is aware of life's countless gifts. To cultivate gratitude is to open a portal to contentment, to find in each moment something worthy of appreciation, to live with a heart that is always ready to be amazed.

The Simple Art of Appreciation

Gratitude begins with a shift in perspective, a willingness to see beyond what is lacking and to focus instead on what is already present. It is the art of appreciating life in its fullness, of recognizing that even in moments of challenge or hardship, there are blessings to be found. Gratitude invites us to see the beauty in the smallest details—a warm bed, a kind word, a simple meal, the sound of laughter.

In a world that often measures worth by what we have, gratitude teaches us to measure by what we appreciate. It reminds us that abundance is not a matter of wealth but of awareness, that happiness lies not in acquiring more but in recognizing the gifts that are already ours. To live with gratitude is to see life as a treasure, each day as an offering, each experience as a chance to say "thank you."

When we approach life with this attitude, we find that even the most ordinary moments become extraordinary. The world takes on a new light, a new vibrancy, as if everything has been touched by grace. And in this shift, we discover a happiness that is deeper, truer, more resilient—a happiness that does not fade with circumstance but grows richer with each day.

Gratitude as a Bridge to Contentment

Contentment is a rare and beautiful state—a quiet,

abiding sense of satisfaction, a feeling that we are enough, that we have enough, that life itself is enough. Gratitude is the bridge that leads us to this place, a path that teaches us to be at peace with what is, to let go of the constant yearning for more, and to find fulfilment in the simple, the present, the now.

Imagine, for a moment, a life lived in contentment —a life where each day is greeted with a sense of appreciation, where each moment is seen as a gift, where happiness is not something to be achieved but something to be experienced. This is the life that gratitude makes possible. It reminds us that happiness is not waiting in some distant future; it is here, in the present, in the things we so often overlook.

Through gratitude, we learn that contentment is not a state of settling but a state of celebrating. It is the realization that our lives, just as they are, are filled with blessings, with beauty, with enoughness. In gratitude, we find the peace of knowing that we do not need more to be happy; we simply need to appreciate what we already have.

Stories of Grateful Hearts

Throughout history, there are countless stories of individuals who have found joy in gratitude, who have faced even the darkest moments with a heart full of appreciation. There is the story of Helen Keller, who, though deaf and blind, expressed a profound gratitude for life and its simple pleasures. For her, every touch, every scent, every memory was a miracle, a reminder that life itself was a gift beyond measure.

And then there is Viktor Frankl, a Holocaust survivor who found meaning and resilience even amidst unimaginable suffering. Through gratitude, he discovered that no matter how dire the circumstances, one could still find something to appreciate, something to hold on to, something to live for. In his gratitude, he found a strength that transcended his suffering, a purpose that illuminated his path.

These stories remind us that gratitude is neither a luxury nor depends on ease or comfort. It is a choice, a practice, a way of seeing that transforms our experience, gives us courage in hardship, and allows us to find light in the darkest of places. Through gratitude, we learn that happiness is not about what we have but about how we see, appreciate, and love.

Practical Exercises in Cultivating Gratitude

Gratitude, like any other virtue, grows stronger with practice. It is a habit of the heart, a way of thinking that must be nurtured, developed, tended to with care. Below are a few simple exercises that can help in cultivating a grateful heart, each one a small step toward a life filled with appreciation and joy.

1. The Gratitude Journal: Each day, take a few moments to write down three things you are grateful for. They can be as simple as the sound of birds in the morning, a good meal, or a moment of laughter. Over time, this practice trains the mind to focus on the positive, to see the blessings in every day, to find joy in the little things.

2. Thank You Notes: Make it a habit to write thank you notes—not only for gifts or favours but for presence, for

kindness, for friendship. Expressing gratitude directly to others deepens the feeling of appreciation, strengthens connections, and brings joy to both the giver and receiver.

3. Mindful Appreciation: Throughout the day, pause to appreciate your surroundings. Notice the colours, the textures, the sounds. Take a moment to feel gratitude for the air you breathe, the ground beneath your feet, the warmth of the sun. This practice helps to cultivate a deep sense of connection to the world, a reminder that we are surrounded by gifts.

4. Gratitude Reflection: Before you go to sleep, take a few moments to reflect on the day and to give thanks for the experiences you had, the lessons learned, the people you encountered. This simple practice closes the day with a heart full of gratitude, preparing you to wake with a spirit of appreciation.

5. A Grateful Heart Meditation: Begin or end your day with a meditation focused on gratitude. Close your eyes, breathe deeply, and bring to mind the things you are grateful for. Allow this feeling of gratitude to fill you, to radiate from your heart, to surround you with a sense of peace.

The Transformative Power of Gratitude

Gratitude transforms. It shifts our focus from scarcity to abundance, from dissatisfaction to contentment, from worry to peace. When we live with gratitude, we become more resilient, more compassionate, more joyful. We learn to see the beauty in all things, to find happiness not in the pursuit of more but in the appreciation of what already is.

Through gratitude, we open ourselves to life in all its fullness. We learn to let go of comparisons, to release the need for perfection, to embrace the imperfection and impermanence that make life so beautiful. Gratitude allows us to live with a sense of wonder, a sense of grace, a sense of belonging to a world filled with countless gifts.

As we continue this journey, let us carry with us a grateful heart, a heart that sees beauty in the ordinary, that finds joy in the small, that is content with the enoughness of life. For in gratitude, we find a happiness that is steady, that is lasting, that is as constant as the love we hold within.

May we live with eyes that see the blessings in each day, with hearts that are ready to give thanks, with spirits that are at peace with what is. And in this way, may we discover that happiness is not something we must chase, but something we can choose, each day, through the simple, sacred act of gratitude.

CHAPTER 6:
RESILIENCE –
THE ART OF
BOUNCING BACK

There is a unique beauty in resilience—a strength that lies not in resistance to life's storms, but in the capacity to rise after each fall, to transform hardship into wisdom, to find grace amidst the trials. Resilience is the quiet power that resides within each of us, a wellspring of courage and endurance, a reminder that we are capable of weathering even the fiercest tempests. It is the art of bouncing back, of bending but not breaking, of growing not despite adversity, but because of it.

Resilience is not simply a trait; it is a journey, an evolution, a becoming. It is the process of forging strength in the fires of experience, of discovering depths within ourselves that we never knew existed. In resilience, we find a pathway to happiness that is not shallow or fleeting, but profound and enduring— a happiness that is strengthened by struggle, a joy that persists even in the face of life's greatest challenges. For resilience teaches us that happiness is not about avoiding pain, but about transcending it, transforming it, using it as a stepping stone to a deeper, richer life.

The Strength of the Willow: Bending Without Breaking

Imagine the willow tree, its branches soft yet strong, bending with the wind, yielding to the storm, yet never breaking. The willow is resilient not because it is unyielding, but because it knows when to bend, when to sway, when to adapt. It is this flexibility, this willingness to move with life's forces, that makes the willow a symbol of resilience—a reminder that strength is not rigidity, but adaptability.

In our own lives, resilience asks us to be like the willow, to find strength not in resisting change, but in flowing with it, in trusting that we have the inner resources to withstand whatever life may bring. When we face hardships, resilience invites us to soften, to yield, to find our balance within the chaos. It teaches us that we need not fight against the storm, but rather learn to dance with it, to let it shape us, to allow it to reveal the strength we carry within.

This is the gift of resilience—a strength that does not come from hardness, but from softness, from an openness to life's challenges, from a willingness to bend but not break. For in each moment of yielding, we discover a deeper power, a resilience that transforms struggle into growth, pain into wisdom, loss into renewal.

Stories of Resilience: Triumph Over Adversity

Throughout history, there have been countless stories of individuals who have faced unimaginable hardship and yet emerged stronger, wiser, more compassionate. These stories remind us that resilience is not about never falling, but about rising again and again, about finding meaning even in the darkest moments, about using adversity as a catalyst for transformation.

One such story is that of Nelson Mandela, who endured 27 years of imprisonment, yet emerged with a heart full of forgiveness, a mind committed to justice, and a vision of peace that would change a nation. Mandela's resilience was not born from bitterness, but from a deep sense of purpose, a belief that even in suffering, one can find meaning, one can choose love over hate, one can rise above the circumstances of life.

And then there is the story of Helen Keller, who, though blind and deaf, saw and heard more beauty in the world than many of us with full senses. Through resilience, she transcended her limitations, finding joy in the simplest experiences, beauty in the smallest wonders, a purpose that inspired millions. Her life is a testament to the power of resilience—a reminder that we are capable of far more than we know, that even in our darkest moments, we can find light.

These stories, like beacons, guide us toward our own resilience. They show us that no matter what challenges we face, we have within us a strength that cannot be extinguished, a spirit that endures, a heart that is capable of boundless love. Resilience is not the absence of suffering, but the presence of hope, of courage, of the will to keep moving forward, even when the path is difficult.

The Science of Resilience: Building Strength Through Adversity

Resilience is not only a poetic ideal; it is a science, a field of study that reveals the incredible capacity of the human mind and body to adapt, to heal, to grow. Research in positive psychology shows that resilience is not an innate quality but a skill that can be developed, a mindset that can be cultivated, a strength that can be nurtured.

The brain, in its remarkable adaptability, responds to challenges by forming new connections, by rewiring itself to cope with stress, by developing pathways that enhance our capacity for endurance. This phenomenon, known as neuroplasticity, reveals that resilience is not a static trait but a dynamic process—a journey of becoming, a constant evolution of self.

In moments of struggle, the brain releases chemicals like dopamine and endorphins, natural substances that reduce pain and increase our sense of reward, enabling us to face challenges with courage and hope. These biochemical processes are the body's way of supporting resilience, of reminding us that we are not alone, that we have within us the resources to face adversity.

But resilience is more than biology; it is also psychology—a mindset that shapes how we see the world, how we interpret events, how we respond to life's difficulties. Studies show that individuals who view challenges as opportunities for growth, who believe in their own capacity to overcome, who maintain a sense of purpose and meaning, are more resilient, more capable of bouncing back, more likely to find joy even in hardship.

Resilience as a Path to Joy

Resilience, at its core, is a pathway to joy—a joy that is

not dependent on circumstance, a happiness that does not fade in the face of difficulty. For when we learn to embrace life's challenges, when we find meaning in our struggles, when we allow adversity to shape us, we discover a joy that is deep, abiding, resilient. This is the joy of a life well-lived, a life that has faced storms and emerged stronger, a life that has found beauty even in brokenness.

Through resilience, we learn that happiness is not the absence of pain, but the presence of courage. It is the strength to keep moving forward, to keep seeking beauty, to keep believing in the goodness of life, even when the path is uncertain. In resilience, we find a happiness that is not fragile, but unbreakable—a joy that is forged in the fires of experience, a contentment that endures.

Practices for Cultivating Resilience

Resilience, like gratitude, is a skill that grows with practice. Below are exercises designed to strengthen resilience, to build the mental and emotional muscles that allow us to bounce back, to find growth in every challenge, to live with courage and joy.

1. Reframing Challenges: When faced with a difficulty, practice reframing it as an opportunity for growth. Ask yourself, "What can I learn from this experience? How can this challenge make me stronger, wiser, more compassionate?" This simple shift in perspective transforms obstacles into stepping stones, enabling you to find meaning in adversity.

2. Mindful Breathing: In moments of stress, take a few deep breaths, focusing on the rise and fall of your breath.

This practice calms the mind, centres the spirit, and reminds you of your own strength, your own resilience, your own capacity to endure.

3. Gratitude for Challenges: Each day, take a moment to express gratitude for a challenge you faced, for a lesson learned, for a hardship that taught you something valuable. This practice fosters resilience by reminding you that even in struggle, there is beauty, there is growth, there is grace.

4. Self-Compassion: Resilience is not about being hard on yourself; it is about being gentle, about allowing yourself to feel, to grieve, to heal. Practice self-compassion by speaking kindly to yourself, by recognizing that resilience is not the absence of struggle but the presence of hope.

5. Visualization of Strength: Imagine yourself as the willow, bending but unbreaking, facing the storm with grace, finding strength in flexibility, courage in softness. This visualization strengthens resilience by reminding you of your inner strength, of the quiet power that resides within.

The Wisdom of Resilience

Resilience is more than a response to hardship; it is a way of being, a way of living with grace, with strength, with an openness to whatever life may bring. It is the wisdom of knowing that happiness is not a destination but a journey, that each challenge, each setback, each moment of pain is an opportunity to grow, to learn, to become.

Through resilience, we learn that life's storms do not diminish us; they refine us. They shape us into beings of strength, of beauty, of depth. They teach us that happiness is not fragile, that joy is not fleeting, that contentment is found not in ease but in the courage to face each day with hope, with love, with an unbreakable spirit.

As we continue this journey, may we carry with us the gift of resilience, the knowledge that we are stronger than we know, that we are capable of facing whatever life may bring, that within each of us lies a wellspring of courage, a reservoir of joy, a heart that is always ready to bounce back.

For in resilience, we find not only happiness but a profound, unshakable peace—a peace that knows no fear, that holds no bitterness, that sees each moment as a chance to grow, to love, to live fully. And in this peace, we discover the true essence of a joyful life.

CHAPTER 7: THE ECSTASY OF FLOW – BECOMING ONE WITH THE MOMENT

There exists a state of being so profound, so absorbing, that the world around us fades into quietness, time slows to a gentle hum, and we become one with the moment, dissolved into pure presence. This state is known as "flow"—a timeless dance of immersion and purpose, a condition where we lose ourselves entirely in the task at hand, our awareness narrowed yet heightened, focused yet expansive. In flow, we experience an ecstasy that is not loud or fleeting, but deep, soulful, enduring—a joy that comes from the heart of creation itself.

Flow is a gift, a rare and beautiful encounter with the present, a place where thoughts cease to chatter, where worries dissolve, where we feel a boundless energy that propels us forward, effortlessly and freely. When we are in flow, we are no longer separate from the task before us; we become it, woven into the fabric of the moment, inseparable from the action, attuned to the rhythm of life itself.

In this chapter, we explore the nature of flow, its profound effects on happiness, and the ways in which we can cultivate this state of total engagement. For in flow, we find not only joy but meaning, a sense of purpose, a feeling of being truly alive. It is here, in this state of immersion, that we touch the essence of happiness, that we experience life not as a series of tasks to be completed, but as a journey to be fully lived.

The Anatomy of Flow: Total Immersion in the Moment

Flow is a state that transcends ordinary consciousness. It is a condition of absolute focus, where we are so deeply engaged in what we are doing that we lose our sense of self, our awareness of time, our thoughts of past and future. In flow, there is no distraction, no hesitation—only the pure, unbroken movement of thought, action, and presence. We are not separate from our work; we are fused with it, part of a seamless dance of creativity and concentration.

This state of flow is marked by a feeling of effortless energy, a sense that everything is aligned, that each action leads naturally into the next, that there is a rhythm and grace to our movements, to our thoughts. The barriers between self and task dissolve, and we become a vessel for the moment, a channel for the joy that arises from pure engagement.

Flow is not something that can be forced or commanded; it is a state that we enter willingly, a condition that arises when the challenge before us is balanced with our skill, when we are stretched but not overwhelmed, when we are focused but not tense. It is a delicate balance, a harmonious meeting of effort and ease, of intention and surrender.

The Joy of Creation: Finding Flow in Art and Craft

Flow is often most readily found in acts of creation—in the artist's brush moving across canvas, in the musician's fingers dancing over strings, in the writer's pen gliding across paper. These moments of creativity, of bringing something new into the world, are fertile grounds for flow. In the act of creation, we become deeply attuned to the present, absorbed in the process, connected to the mystery of creation itself.

For the artist, flow is a place of magic, a state where ideas come effortlessly, where inspiration flows like a river, where the self dissolves and all that remains is the work, the creation, the moment of expression. In these moments, we are no longer bound by the limits of our own minds; we are free, open, expansive. We feel a joy that is not tied to the outcome of our efforts, but to the process itself, to the act of bringing something new into being.

This is the joy of creation, the ecstasy of flow— a happiness that is not dependent on success or achievement, but on the simple, profound pleasure of creating, of expressing, of being fully engaged in the process of bringing beauty into the world.

Flow in Movement: The Dance of Body and Mind

Flow is not limited to the creative arts; it can be found

in any activity that fully engages the body and mind. Athletes experience flow in the midst of competition, runners feel it as they find their stride, dancers lose themselves in the rhythm, moving in harmony with the music. In these moments, there is no separation between the body and the mind; they are one, moving together, attuned to the same rhythm, the same pulse of energy.

In the flow of movement, we experience a freedom that is both physical and mental. Our bodies move effortlessly, guided by instinct, by intuition, by a deeper wisdom that lies beyond conscious thought. We feel alive, vibrant, powerful, connected to something greater than ourselves. In this state, there is no room for doubt or hesitation; there is only the pure, unbroken flow of energy, the joy of being fully present in the body, fully engaged in the moment.

This is the ecstasy of flow—a happiness that arises not from accomplishment, but from presence, from the simple act of being in motion, of living fully in the now. It is a happiness that is not bound by success or failure, but by the experience of total immersion, by the joy of being alive, of feeling the pulse of life moving through us.

Cultivating Flow in Daily Life: Finding Joy in Engagement

Flow is not limited to extraordinary moments or creative pursuits; it can be cultivated in the ordinary tasks of daily life. We can find flow in washing dishes, in gardening, in cooking, in any activity that invites our full attention, that allows us to be present, to lose ourselves in the task at hand.

The key to finding flow in everyday life is to

approach each task with intention, with curiosity, with a willingness to be fully engaged. When we bring mindfulness to even the simplest activities, we create the conditions for flow. We let go of distractions, we focus on the task before us, we allow ourselves to be absorbed in the rhythm of the moment.

Imagine, for a moment, the act of preparing a meal. There is a joy in chopping vegetables, in watching the ingredients come together, in feeling the warmth of the stove, in tasting the flavours as they blend. In these moments, we are not simply preparing food; we are engaged in a ritual, a process of creation, a moment of connection to the present. And in this engagement, we find a happiness that is quiet, simple, profound—a happiness that comes not from the result, but from the act itself.

The Benefits of Flow: Happiness, Fulfilment, Meaning

Flow is more than a fleeting experience of joy; it is a state that brings profound benefits to our well-being, our happiness, our sense of purpose. When we experience flow, we feel a deep sense of fulfilment, a feeling that we are living fully, that we are engaged in something meaningful. Flow gives us a respite from the constant noise of the mind, from the worries and doubts that often cloud our thoughts. It allows us to be present, to be at peace, to find joy in the simple act of being.

Research in positive psychology shows that flow is closely associated with happiness, with a sense of purpose, with an overall feeling of well-being. People who regularly experience flow are more likely to feel fulfilled, to find joy in their work, to feel connected to their passions. Flow is a pathway to happiness that is not dependent on external rewards or accomplishments; it is a happiness that arises from within, from the simple pleasure of being fully engaged in life.

In flow, we find a happiness that is free from the need for approval, for success, for recognition. We find a joy that is self-sustaining, a contentment that is rooted in the present, a fulfilment that does not fade with time. This is the joy of flow—a happiness that is as pure and natural as the breath, as steady and enduring as the heartbeat.

Practices for Entering Flow: Cultivating Presence and Focus

Flow is a state that can be cultivated, a condition that we can invite into our lives through practice, through intention, through a willingness to be present. Below are exercises that can help in cultivating flow, that can create the conditions for this profound experience of total immersion, that can guide us toward a happiness that is rooted in presence, in purpose, in the simple joy of being.

1. Choose Activities with Meaning: Flow is most easily found in activities that hold meaning for us, that resonate with our passions, our interests, our values. Choose activities that engage you, that challenge you, that bring you joy, and allow yourself to be fully present in them.

2. Set Clear Goals: Flow arises when there is a balance between challenge and skill, when we are stretched but not overwhelmed. Set clear goals for yourself, goals that are achievable yet engaging, that allow you to focus, to immerse yourself in the task at hand.

3. Limit Distractions: Flow requires focus, a concentration that is undisturbed by outside distractions. Create a space for yourself that is free from interruptions, a space where you can be fully present, fully engaged, fully in the moment.

4. Practice Mindfulness: Flow is closely related to mindfulness, to the ability to be present, to focus on the here and now. Practice mindfulness in your daily life, in your routines, in your interactions, and allow this presence to guide you into the state of flow.

5. Embrace the Process: Flow is about the journey, not the destination. Allow yourself to be absorbed in the process, to find joy in each step, to be content with the act of doing, with the experience of being.

The Joy of Flow: A Gateway to True Happiness

Flow is a doorway to happiness, a gateway to a state of being that is free, expansive, joyful. It is a place where we find ourselves, where we lose ourselves, where we experience life not as a series of moments to be managed, but as a journey to be savoured, a dance to be enjoyed, a song to be sung.

In flow, we touch a happiness that is deeper than pleasure, that is more lasting than excitement, that is as simple and profound as the present moment. For in flow, we find the essence of life, the joy of being, the ecstasy of becoming one with the moment.

As we continue this journey, may we seek out the moments that bring us to flow, that allow us to dissolve into the beauty of the present, that connect us to the heartbeat of life. May we find in flow a happiness that is pure, a joy that is boundless, a contentment that is eternal.

CHAPTER 8: THE SANCTUARY WITHIN – CULTIVATING INNER PEACE

There is a place within each of us, a sanctuary untouched by the noise of the world, a refuge where the soul can rest, the heart can breathe, and the mind can find peace. This sanctuary is not a distant, unreachable haven; it is close, intimate, woven into the fabric of our being. It is a space beyond thought, beyond worry, beyond the demands of daily life—a place of stillness, of quiet, of profound contentment. In this inner sanctuary, we are whole, complete, connected to a deeper essence, a place where true peace resides.

The journey to this sanctuary is not one of distance, but of awareness, of turning inward, of letting go of the distractions and disturbances that pull us away from ourselves. To find peace within is to cultivate an intimacy with our own soul, a gentle relationship with our own mind, a compassionate embrace of our own heart. In this chapter, we explore the art of introspection, the practice of stillness, the beauty of inner peace. For in this sanctuary, we find a happiness that is steady, a joy that is quiet, a contentment that does not waver.

The Path of Introspection: Journeying Inward

Introspection is the first step on the path to inner peace. It is the art of looking within, of gently turning our awareness inward, of observing the landscape of our own mind, our own heart, our own soul. In introspection, we do not judge or criticize; we simply witness, we observe, we listen. We become quiet, receptive, open to whatever arises within us.

To practice introspection is to embark on a journey of self-discovery, a journey that leads us not away from the world, but deeper into ourselves. It is a process of uncovering, of peeling back the layers of thoughts, beliefs, and emotions that cloud our inner peace. In this journey, we begin to understand ourselves more deeply, to see our own patterns, to recognize our own tendencies, to become aware of the subtle ways in which we resist or embrace peace.

Through introspection, we come to realize that peace is not something we must achieve, but something we must remember, something that is already within us, waiting to be acknowledged, to be embraced, to be felt. This awareness is the foundation of inner peace—a reminder that we carry within us all that we need, that we are whole, that we are enough.

The Power of Stillness: Finding Peace in Silence

Stillness is the doorway to our inner sanctuary. In a world that is constantly in motion, where busyness is often mistaken for purpose, stillness is a radical act, a return to simplicity, a quieting of the mind, a softening of the heart. To be still is to be present, to rest in the moment, to let go of the need to do, to accomplish, to achieve. It is an invitation to simply be, to dwell in the silence, to listen to the gentle whispers of our own soul.

Imagine, for a moment, the beauty of stillness—a quiet morning, the world hushed, the air filled with calm, the mind as clear as a tranquil lake. In this stillness, we find a peace that is not dependent on circumstances, a contentment that arises from within, a sense of wholeness that is beyond words. Stillness is a practice, a skill, a way of being that invites us to return to our natural state of peace, to reconnect with the serenity that lies beneath the surface of our thoughts.

To cultivate stillness is to make space for peace, to allow the mind to rest, to let the heart breathe, to give the soul room to simply be. It is a practice of letting go, of releasing the constant need for stimulation, for distraction, for movement. In this letting go, we discover a peace that is gentle, that is calm, that is as steady as the breath, as constant as the heartbeat.

Meditation: The Pathway to Inner Calm

Meditation is the practice of finding our way back to ourselves, a journey inward, a return to the present, a space where we can rest, where we can heal, where we can feel whole. It is a practice that invites us to sit in stillness, to observe without judgment, to allow our thoughts to come and go like clouds in the sky. In meditation, we are not trying to control the mind; we are simply witnessing it, letting it be, allowing it to settle, to quiet, to return to its natural state of peace.

In meditation, we find a peace that is not about silence or emptiness, but about presence, about being fully here, fully alive, fully aware. It is a peace that does not come from escaping the world, but from embracing it, from accepting it, from being with it in a way that is open, compassionate, and gentle. Meditation teaches us that peace is not a destination, but a state of being, a way of living, a way of seeing the world.

To meditate is to practice peace, to cultivate a relationship with our own mind, to learn to be with ourselves in a way that is kind, that is patient, that is loving. Through meditation, we create a sanctuary within, a place where we can return whenever we need, a refuge from the storms of life, a haven of calm, of quiet, of peace.

Breathing as a Balm for the Soul

Breathing is our anchor, our connection to life, our source of calm. It is the simplest, most natural practice, yet it holds within it a profound power, a gateway to peace, a pathway to stillness. To breathe mindfully is to return to the present, to ground ourselves in the now, to let go of the past, to release the future, to simply be with the breath, with the moment, with ourselves.

Imagine, for a moment, the sensation of a deep, slow breath—a breath that fills the lungs, that nourishes the body, that soothes the mind, that brings a sense of calm to the heart. This is the gift of the breath, a gentle reminder that peace is always available, that we can return to it with each inhale, with each exhale, that we can find sanctuary within ourselves.

Breathing is more than a physical act; it is a practice of presence, a meditation in motion, a way of connecting with the peace that resides within. When we breathe mindfully, we create a rhythm of calm, a flow of peace, a sense of grounding that carries us through even the most challenging moments. The breath is a balm for the soul, a source of comfort, a reminder that we are here, that we are alive, that we are connected to the peace within.

Practices for Cultivating Inner Peace

Inner peace is not something that can be attained through force or effort; it is a state of being that arises naturally, that flows from a place of acceptance, of presence, of compassion. Below are gentle practices that can help in cultivating this peace, practices that invite us to turn inward, to create a sanctuary within, to nourish the soul.

1. Daily Reflection: Set aside a few moments each day to sit in quiet reflection. Allow yourself to simply be, to observe your thoughts, to feel your emotions, to be present with whatever arises. This practice helps to cultivate a gentle awareness, a connection to the peace that lies beneath the surface of the mind.

2. Mindful Breathing: Throughout the day, take a few moments to focus on your breath. Feel each inhale, each exhale, allow the breath to flow naturally, to bring a sense of calm to the body, to the mind. This simple practice

is a reminder that peace is always available, that we can return to it with each breath.

3. Body Scan Meditation: Close your eyes and bring your awareness to each part of your body, from the top of your head to the tips of your toes. Notice any tension, any sensation, any feeling, and allow yourself to relax, to release, to let go. This practice helps to cultivate a sense of presence, a connection to the body, a feeling of grounding and peace.

4. Gratitude Practice: Each day, take a moment to reflect on something you are grateful for, something that brings you joy, something that nourishes your soul. Gratitude is a pathway to peace, a way of seeing the beauty in life, a reminder of the abundance that surrounds us.

5. Visualization of a Safe Space: Close your eyes and imagine a place that feels safe, that feels peaceful, that feels like a sanctuary. This place could be real or imagined —a forest, a beach, a garden. Allow yourself to feel the peace of this space, to rest in it, to let it soothe and comfort you. This practice is a reminder that peace is not a distant dream, but a feeling that we can create within ourselves.

The Beauty of Inner Peace

Inner peace is a state of grace, a condition of contentment, a feeling of wholeness that does not waver. It is the quiet assurance that we are enough, that we are whole, that we are connected to something greater than ourselves. In this peace, we find a happiness that is not dependent on what we have, on what we achieve, on what we become. It is a happiness that flows from within, a joy that is as simple and as profound as the breath, as steady as the heartbeat.

To cultivate inner peace is to create a sanctuary within, a place of calm, a place of quiet, a place of rest. It is to find a refuge from the noise, from the demands, from the constant movement of life. In this sanctuary, we are free, we are whole, we are at peace.

As we continue this journey, may we carry with us the gift of inner peace, the knowledge that we have within us all that we need, that we are enough, that we are whole. May we find in this peace a happiness that is steady, a joy that is quiet, a contentment that endures.

In inner peace, we find a sanctuary that is always open, a haven that is always safe, a home that is always within us. And in this peace, we discover the true essence of happiness—a happiness that is gentle, that is kind, that is as constant as the love we hold within.

CHAPTER 9: PURPOSE AS A BEACON – FINDING MEANING IN LIFE

In the vast ocean of human experience, there is a guiding light, a beacon that illuminates our path and gives depth to our journey. This light is purpose—a powerful force that shapes who we are, what we do, and how we experience the world. The purpose is the "why" that brings meaning to our days, the inner compass that directs our steps, the flame that burns steadily within, even through the darkest nights.

Purpose is not merely a goal or a destination; it is a way of being, a way of aligning our lives with something greater, something that resonates deeply within us. When we live with purpose, we find a happiness that is rich, layered, resilient—a happiness that is not swayed by circumstances, but rooted in a profound sense of meaning. In this chapter, we explore the journey of discovering and nurturing our purpose, and how this inner calling serves as a pathway to a truly fulfilled life.

The Search for Meaning: A Timeless Human Quest

The search for meaning is as old as humanity itself. Across cultures and centuries, people have sought answers to the timeless questions: "Why am I here? What is my purpose? What gives my life meaning?" These questions are not a mere intellectual exercise; they are a longing of the soul, a desire to find something that transcends the mundane, that fills our lives with significance, that gives each moment a sense of direction.

This quest for meaning is not a burden but a gift, a journey that invites us to look beyond ourselves, to connect with something larger, to live with a sense of intention. It is this search that brings depth to our lives, that transforms ordinary days into extraordinary ones, that allows us to see each moment as part of a larger story, a story that is uniquely our own.

In our search for purpose, we do not find all the answers at once; rather, we uncover them piece by piece, moment by moment, experience by experience. Purpose is not a destination to be reached, but a path to be walked, a journey that unfolds with each step, a discovery that grows richer, deeper, more meaningful with time.

The Power of "Why": Purpose as a Source of Joy

To have a purpose is to live with a "why," a reason that infuses our actions with meaning, that brings a sense of fulfilment, that fills our days with joy. Purpose gives us something to strive for, something to cherish, something to look forward to. It is the fire that ignites our passions, the force that propels us forward, the foundation upon which we build our lives.

When we know our "why," we approach life with a sense of clarity, with a feeling of empowerment, with a conviction that we are moving in the right direction. Purpose gives us the strength to face challenges, the resilience to overcome obstacles, the courage to pursue our dreams. It reminds us that we are part of something larger, something beautiful, something that matters.

Purpose does not eliminate struggle; rather, it transforms it. With purpose, every setback becomes a lesson, every difficulty an opportunity for growth. We are no longer discouraged by failure, because we know that each experience brings us closer to fulfilling our purpose, to living a life that is true, that is meaningful, that is deeply fulfilling.

Discovering Your Unique Purpose: A Journey Within

Purpose is not something that can be given to us; it is something we must discover, something we must unearth from within. Each of us carries within us a unique purpose, a calling that is ours alone, a reason for being that reflects our deepest values, our truest passions, our highest aspirations. To find this purpose, we must turn inward, we must listen to the quiet voice of the heart, we must allow ourselves to feel, to dream, to imagine.

The journey to discovering our purpose is not always straightforward. It requires patience, introspection, a willingness to explore our own depths, to question our own assumptions, to see ourselves in a new light. Purpose often emerges not from moments of certainty, but from moments of reflection, from times of transition, from experiences that challenge us to grow, to evolve, to become more than we were before.

In this journey, it is helpful to ask ourselves a few guiding questions: What brings me joy? What activities make me feel alive, engaged, fulfilled? What are my core values, the principles that guide my actions and decisions? What legacy do I want to leave behind? By asking these questions, we begin to uncover the threads of our purpose, the elements that give our lives meaning, the pieces of the puzzle that come together to reveal our unique "why."

Aligning Purpose with Action: Living a Life of Meaning

To know our purpose is a powerful thing, but purpose alone is not enough; it must be aligned with action, with intention, with a commitment to live in accordance with our "why." Purpose is not an abstract concept; it is a living, breathing force, a dynamic energy that must be expressed, that must be brought to life through our choices, our actions, our interactions.

When we align our actions with our purpose, we create a life that is coherent, a life that is whole, a life that feels true. Each action, no matter how small, becomes a step in the direction of our purpose, a piece of the larger picture, a brushstroke on the canvas of our lives. In this alignment, we find a happiness that is not superficial, but profound—a happiness that comes from knowing that we are living in harmony with our values, with our dreams, with our highest self.

To live with purpose is not to be free from challenges, but to be free from doubt. It is to know, deep within, that we are on the right path, that each day is an opportunity to live fully, to love deeply, to serve generously. Purpose gives us a sense of direction, a sense of fulfilment, a sense of peace. It is a guiding light, a beacon that leads us through the dark, that gives us the courage to keep moving forward, that fills our lives with meaning.

Stories of Purpose: Lives Guided by "Why"

Throughout history, there have been countless individuals whose lives have been shaped by a profound sense of purpose, a "why" that has guided their actions, that has given them the strength to overcome adversity, that has allowed them to make a difference in the world. These stories inspire us, reminding us of the power of purpose, of the joy that comes from living a life of meaning.

Think of Mahatma Gandhi, a man whose purpose was to bring freedom to his people, to create a world of peace, of justice, of compassion. His purpose was not an easy one; it required sacrifice, resilience, a courage that defied all odds. Yet it was this purpose that gave him strength, that filled him with a sense of joy, a sense of fulfilment, a sense of peace. Through his purpose, he changed the world, leaving behind a legacy of love, of courage, of hope.

Or of Mother Teresa, a woman whose purpose was to serve the poor, the suffering, the forgotten. Her life was not one of comfort or ease; it was a life of service, a life of sacrifice, a life of love. Yet in this purpose, she found a joy that was beyond measure, a happiness that was not of this world, a peace that came from knowing that she was fulfilling her calling, that she was living her "why."

These stories remind us that purpose is not about comfort, but about meaning, not about ease, but about fulfilment. They show us that a life lived with purpose is a life of joy, a life of peace, a life of profound happiness.

Practices for Discovering and Living Your Purpose

Finding and living our purpose is a lifelong journey, a process of exploration, of growth, of alignment. Below are practices that can help us connect with our purpose, that can guide us on the path to a life of meaning, a life of fulfilment, a life of true happiness.

1. Reflection on Values: Take time to reflect on your core values, the principles that matter most to you, the beliefs that guide your actions. Write them down, let them guide your decisions, let them serve as a foundation for your purpose.

2. Passion Exploration: Make a list of the activities, the causes, the ideas that ignite your passion, that make you feel alive, that bring you joy. These passions are often clues to your purpose, to the unique contribution you are here to make.

3. Visualization of Legacy: Imagine yourself at the end of your life, looking back on your journey. What do you hope to have accomplished? What legacy do you wish to leave? This exercise can bring clarity to your purpose, revealing the impact you want to make, the life you want to live.

4. Purpose in Daily Action: Purpose is not only about grand achievements; it is about living each day with intention, with presence, with a commitment to align our actions with our values. Each day, ask yourself, "How

can I live my purpose today? How can I bring meaning to this moment?"

5. Service to Others: Purpose often emerges through service, through acts of kindness, through contributions that uplift others. Look for ways to serve, to give, to make a difference. In this service, you may find the seeds of your purpose, a joy that comes from connection, from compassion, from love.

Purpose as a Source of Happiness

Purpose is a source of happiness that does not fade, a joy that does not waver, a contentment that is as steady as the stars, as enduring as the earth. It is a happiness that arises from within, from the knowledge that we are living a life of meaning, a life of value, a life that is true to who we are. Purpose is not a destination, but a journey, a journey that brings us closer to ourselves, to others, to the world.

As we continue this journey, may we carry with us the gift of purpose, the light of our "why," the knowledge that we are here for a reason, that our lives have meaning, that each day is an opportunity to live with intention, with love, with joy.

In purpose, we find a deep happiness, a joy that is true, an unshakable contentment. And in this purpose, we discover the true essence of a fulfilled life—a life guided by love, by meaning, by the quiet, steady light of our own unique "why."

CHAPTER 10: EMBRACING VULNERABILITY – THE STRENGTH IN OPENNESS

There is a quiet power in vulnerability, a strength that lies not in the armour we wear, but in the courage to stand unguarded, to be seen, to be known. Vulnerability is not a weakness; it is the willingness to be open, to be real, to show up in life as we truly are, with all our imperfections, all our dreams, all our fears. In vulnerability, we find a path to freedom, a way of living that is authentic, a way of being that is true.

To be vulnerable is to embrace the full spectrum of our humanity, to honour both our strengths and our struggles, to live without hiding, without pretending, without the need to be anything other than who we are. It is to step into the world with an open heart, to risk being hurt, being judged, being misunderstood, in the hope of finding connection, of experiencing love, of building a life that is meaningful, that is rich, that is real.

In this chapter, we explore vulnerability as a source of strength, as a doorway to happiness, as a bridge that connects us to ourselves and to others. For in vulnerability, we discover the beauty of authenticity, the joy of connection, the freedom that comes from living a life that is open, that is honest, that is deeply, beautifully human.

The Myths of Vulnerability: Breaking Free from Fear

In a world that often prizes strength, independence, and self-sufficiency, vulnerability is sometimes seen as a flaw, as a sign of weakness, as something to be avoided. We are taught to be tough, to be resilient, to hide our insecurities, our doubts, our fears. Yet this view of vulnerability is based on a misunderstanding, a myth that blinds us to its true power, its true beauty, its true purpose.

Vulnerability is not about weakness; it is about courage. It is the courage to be seen, to be known, to show up in life without hiding, without pretending, without the need for perfection. It is the strength to face our own humanity, to accept our own imperfections, to live with an open heart, even when we fear the risk of being hurt.

To be vulnerable is to be real, to be honest, to be authentic. It is to let go of the need to impress, to be flawless, to be invulnerable. It is to embrace the truth of who we are, to stand in our own skin, to live with a heart that is open, a spirit that is free, a soul that is whole. This is the strength of vulnerability—a strength that does not come from hiding our fears, but from facing them, from embracing them, from allowing them to be a part of our journey.

The Freedom of Authenticity: Embracing Our True Selves

There is a profound freedom that comes from authenticity, a liberation that arises when we allow ourselves to be who we truly are, without masks, without pretence, without the need for approval. To live authentically is to honour our own truth, to follow our own path, to speak our own voice. It is to embrace our uniqueness, our individuality, our own beautiful, imperfect, one-of-a-kind self.

Authenticity is not about being perfect; it is about being real. It is the courage to say, "This is who I am," without apology, without shame, without the need to be anything other than ourselves. It is to live in a way that is true, that is honest, that is aligned with our own values, our own beliefs, our own heart.

When we embrace authenticity, we find a happiness that is not dependent on external validation, a joy that is not swayed by the opinions of others, a contentment that is rooted in self-acceptance. We are free from the need to be someone we are not, free from the pressure to meet others' expectations, free to live a life that is uniquely, beautifully our own.

In this freedom, we find a happiness that is deep, a peace that is lasting, a strength that is unshakable. For to live authentically is to live with integrity, to live in alignment with our true self, to live a life that is whole, that is real, that is full.

The Power of Connection: Building Bridges Through Openness

Vulnerability is the foundation of connection, the bridge that brings us closer to others, the pathway that allows us to experience true intimacy, true love, true belonging. When we are vulnerable, we open ourselves to others, we allow them to see us, to know us, to understand us. We create a space for connection, for empathy, for compassion.

To be vulnerable with others is to invite them into our lives, to share our joys, our sorrows, our dreams, our fears. It is to say, "I am here, I am open, I am willing to be seen." In this openness, we create a bond that is real, a connection that is deep, a relationship that is built on trust, on understanding, on shared humanity.

Through vulnerability, we find a happiness that is not solitary, but shared, a joy that is enriched by the presence of others, a contentment that is magnified by connection. For when we are open, we are no longer alone; we are part of a community, a family, a circle of love. In this connection, we find a happiness that is full, a love that is true, a sense of belonging that is profound.

The Courage to Be Open: Stepping into Vulnerability

Vulnerability requires courage, a willingness to step into the unknown, a readiness to take risks, a strength that comes from within. It is not easy to be open, to share our true selves, to let others see our imperfections, our insecurities, our doubts. Yet it is this courage, this willingness to be open, that brings us closer to happiness, to fulfilment, to peace.

When we embrace vulnerability, we learn to live with a heart that is open, a heart that is ready to give and receive love, a heart that is free from fear. We learn to let go of the need for perfection, to release the pressure to be invulnerable, to accept ourselves as we are. We find a strength that is not about being flawless, but about being real, about being human, about being whole.

This is the gift of vulnerability—a gift that brings us closer to ourselves, to others, to the world. For in vulnerability, we find the courage to live fully, to love deeply, to be truly alive.

Stories of Strength in Vulnerability

Throughout history, there are stories of individuals who have embraced vulnerability, who have found strength in openness, who have discovered the beauty of authenticity. These stories remind us of the power of vulnerability, of the joy that comes from living with an open heart, of the freedom that arises when we are true to ourselves.

Consider the story of Maya Angelou, a poet, a writer, a woman who lived with courage, with authenticity, with a heart that was open to the world. Through her words, she shared her truth, her struggles, her triumphs, her dreams. She was vulnerable, she was real, she was honest. And through her vulnerability, she found a strength that inspired millions, a joy that came from being true to herself, a peace that arose from living a life of authenticity.

Or take the story of Brené Brown, a researcher, a storyteller, a woman who has dedicated her life to understanding the power of vulnerability. Through her work, she has shown us that vulnerability is not a weakness, but a strength, a source of connection, a pathway to happiness. She has taught us that to be vulnerable is to be brave, to be real, to be human.

These stories remind us that vulnerability is not something to be feared, but something to be embraced, something to be celebrated, something to be honoured. They show us that a life lived with vulnerability is a life of courage, a life of joy, a life of meaning.

Practices for Embracing Vulnerability

Embracing vulnerability is a practice, a journey, a way of living that requires intention, that calls for courage, that invites us to be open. Below are practices that can help us embrace vulnerability, that can guide us on the path to a life of authenticity, a life of connection, a life of true happiness.

1. Practice Self-Acceptance: Begin by accepting yourself as you are, with all your strengths, all your weaknesses, all your dreams, all your fears. Embrace your own humanity, honour your own journey, be kind to yourself. Self-acceptance is the foundation of vulnerability, a reminder that you are enough, just as you are.

2. Share Your Truth: Practice sharing your truth with others, whether it is a fear, a hope, a dream, a feeling. Allow yourself to be seen, to be known, to be understood. This practice helps to build connection, to create intimacy, to foster empathy.

3. Release Perfectionism: Let go of the need to be perfect, to be flawless, to be invulnerable. Embrace your imperfections, honour your mistakes, celebrate your uniqueness. Perfectionism is the enemy of vulnerability;

to be vulnerable is to be real, to be authentic, to be human.

4. Be Open to Receiving: Vulnerability is not only about giving; it is also about receiving, about allowing others to support us, to love us, to understand us. Practice being open to the love and kindness of others, practice accepting help, practice receiving with gratitude.

5. Reflect on Moments of Openness: Take time to reflect on moments when you were open, when you were vulnerable, when you allowed yourself to be seen. Notice how these moments made you feel, notice the connection they created, notice the joy they brought. This reflection helps to reinforce the power of vulnerability, to remind you of its beauty, to inspire you to embrace it.

The Joy of Vulnerability: A Path to True Happiness

Vulnerability is a path to happiness that is not about avoiding pain, but about embracing it, about living with a heart that is open, a spirit that is free, a soul that is whole. It is a happiness that is not based on perfection, but on authenticity, a joy that arises not from invulnerability, but from courage, a contentment that is rooted in love, in connection, in truth.

As we continue this journey, may we carry with us the gift of vulnerability, the knowledge that we are strong not because we are flawless, but because we are real. May we find in vulnerability a pathway to happiness, a doorway to love, a source of strength.

In vulnerability, we find the freedom to be ourselves, the courage to be open, the joy of living a true life. And in this openness, we discover the true essence of happiness—a happiness that is gentle, that is kind, that is as deep as the love we hold within.

CHAPTER 11: ACTS OF KINDNESS – THE ALTRUISTIC PATH TO JOY

In the quiet beauty of kindness, there is a power that transforms both the giver and the receiver, a light that brightens the world, a joy that transcends the boundaries of self. Acts of kindness, no matter how small, are gifts not only to others but to ourselves—a gesture, a smile, a moment of compassion that ripples outward, touching lives in ways we may never fully see, fully know, or fully understand. Kindness is a language of the heart, a bridge that connects us to others, a doorway to a happiness that is deep, lasting, and profoundly fulfilling.

To be kind is to step out of the narrow confines of the self, to reach beyond our own needs, our own desires, our own lives. It is an act of openness, of generosity, of love. And in this openness, we find a happiness that is greater than anything we could achieve alone, a joy that is shared, a contentment that comes from knowing that we have made a difference, that we have touched a life, that we have been a force for good.

In this chapter, we explore kindness as an altruistic path to joy, a way of finding happiness through connection, through compassion, through the simple, beautiful act of giving. For in kindness, we discover a happiness that is not fleeting, but steady, not shallow, but profound—a happiness that is rooted in love, in empathy, in the joy of uplifting others.

The Power of Small Gestures: Transformative Acts of Kindness

Kindness does not always come in grand gestures or life-changing actions; often, it is found in the smallest moments, the simplest acts, the quiet exchanges that fill our days. A smile shared with a stranger, a hand extended in friendship, a word of encouragement, a listening ear— these are the acts of kindness that weave the fabric of our lives, that remind us of our shared humanity, that create a world where love, compassion, and understanding prevail.

These small gestures may seem insignificant, but their effects are profound. Research in positive psychology shows that acts of kindness have a ripple effect, that each kind act inspires others to do the same, that each moment of compassion spreads like light, illuminating the lives it touches. Kindness is contagious, a force that grows, that multiplies, that transforms. And in this transformation, we find not only a happier world but a happier self, a self that is enriched, fulfilled, connected.

To give kindness is to receive joy, to create a happiness that is shared, a love that is given freely, a peace that is found in connection. For in these small acts of kindness, we discover that happiness is not about what we have, but about what we give, about the difference we make, about the love we share.

The Science of Kindness: Altruism and Happiness

Science has long confirmed what human wisdom has always known—that acts of kindness are not only good for the soul, but for the mind and body as well. Studies in psychology and neuroscience reveal that when we engage in acts of kindness, our brains release "feel-good" chemicals like dopamine and oxytocin, which create a sense of pleasure, of well-being, of connection. This phenomenon, often called the "helper's high," shows us that kindness is not only beneficial for others but profoundly nourishing for ourselves.

In one study, researchers found that individuals who regularly engage in acts of kindness report higher levels of happiness, greater life satisfaction, and lower levels of stress and anxiety. Another study showed that even small acts of kindness, like holding the door open for someone or offering a kind word, can improve our mood, increase our sense of connection, and boost our overall well-being.

These findings reveal a simple truth: kindness is a pathway to happiness, a way of elevating our own lives by uplifting others, a source of joy that arises not from what we receive but from what we give. Kindness connects us, it heals us, it brings us closer to ourselves and to others, creating a sense of purpose, a feeling of fulfilment, a happiness that is shared, that is multiplied, that is real.

Stories of Kindness: Lives Transformed by Compassion

Throughout history, there are stories of individuals

whose acts of kindness have changed lives, whose compassion has created ripples that extend far beyond themselves. These stories remind us of the power of kindness, of the joy that comes from giving, of the beauty that arises when we live with a heart that is open, a spirit that is generous, a soul that is kind.

Consider the story of Oseola McCarty, a humble washerwoman who spent her life saving pennies, dimes, and dollars from her small income. When she retired, Oseola, who had never earned more than a modest living, donated $150,000 to the University of Southern Mississippi to fund scholarships for deserving students. Her act of kindness, born of a life of simplicity and generosity, changed the lives of countless young people, creating opportunities, opening doors, spreading hope. Through her kindness, Oseola found a joy that was deep, a peace that was lasting, a fulfilment that went beyond material wealth.

Or take the story of Dr Patch Adams, a physician who dedicated his life to bringing joy to patients through humour, compassion, and kindness. Dr Adams believed that healing was not only a matter of medicine, but of love, of connection, of laughter. His kindness transformed lives, uplifted spirits, brought light to those in darkness. His life is a testament to the power of kindness, a reminder that happiness is not about what we receive, but about what we give, about the love we share, about the joy we bring to others.

These stories inspire us to be kind, to live with a heart that is open, to see each day as an opportunity to make a difference, to bring light, to spread love. For in these acts of kindness, we find a happiness that is true, a joy that is full, a life that is deeply, profoundly fulfilled.

Cultivating a Kind Heart: Practices for Altruistic Joy

Kindness is not only an action; it is a way of being, a way of moving through the world with compassion, with generosity, with love. Below are practices that can help us cultivate a kind heart, that can guide us on the path of altruistic joy, that can create a life that is rich in connection, in meaning, in happiness.

1. Random Acts of Kindness: Practice kindness spontaneously, without expectation, without planning, without the need for recognition. Leave a kind note for someone, pay for a stranger's coffee, offer a compliment, lend a helping hand. These small acts of kindness are gifts, a reminder that love is found in the everyday, in the simple, in the ordinary.

2. Practice Active Listening: Kindness is not only about giving but about being present, about listening, about understanding. Practice active listening with those around you, offering your full attention, your empathy, your compassion. This practice helps to create a connection, to build trust, to foster love.

3. Volunteer Your Time: Find a cause that resonates with you, a way to serve, a way to give back. Volunteering is a way of connecting with others, of making a difference, of finding joy through service. It is a reminder that kindness is not only an action but a way of living, a way of being.

4. Express Gratitude for Others: Take time to express gratitude for the kindness of others, to acknowledge the love, the support, the compassion that surrounds you. This practice of gratitude helps to cultivate a sense

of connection, a feeling of appreciation, a happiness that arises from the knowledge that we are part of a community, a family, a circle of love.

5. Reflect on the Impact of Kindness: At the end of each day, take a moment to reflect on the acts of kindness you gave and received. Notice the effect they had on you, the joy they brought, the connection they created. This reflection helps to reinforce the power of kindness, to remind you of its beauty, to inspire you to live with a heart that is open, a spirit that is kind.

The Joy of Giving: A Happiness That is Shared

Kindness is a path to joy, a way of finding happiness through connection, through compassion, through the simple, beautiful act of giving. It is a happiness that is not solitary, but shared, a joy that is not fleeting, but lasting, a peace that is not shallow, but profound. For in kindness, we find a happiness that is true, a joy that is full, a contentment that arises from love, from generosity, from connection.

As we continue this journey, may we carry with us the gift of kindness, the knowledge that we have the power to make a difference, to bring light, to spread love. May we find in kindness a path to happiness, a source of joy, a way of living that is meaningful, that is rich, that is real.

In kindness, we discover the true essence of happiness—a happiness that is not found in what we have, but in what we give, a joy that is not about receiving, but about sharing, a contentment that is as deep as the love we hold within.

CHAPTER 12: THE SYMPHONY OF RELATIONSHIPS – BUILDING EMOTIONAL BONDS

In the symphony of life, relationships are the melody that weaves through every note, every chord, every beat. They are the harmonies that give depth to our experiences, the rhythms that connect us to one another, the notes that linger, that resonate, that stay. Relationships are the bridges that span the spaces between us, the threads that bind us to the world, the light that brightens even the darkest days. In the beauty of human connection, we find not only happiness but a sense of belonging, of being seen, of being loved.

To love and to be loved is to experience life in its fullness, to feel the heartbeat of another as your own, to recognize yourself in the eyes of another, to know that you are not alone. Relationships are the mirror in which we see ourselves, the canvas upon which we paint our hopes, our dreams, our fears. Through connection, we find meaning, we find joy, we find a happiness that is shared, a contentment that is deep, a love that is as boundless as the sky.

In this chapter, we explore relationships as a source of happiness, as a foundation of well-being, as a symphony of emotions, of memories, of moments that bind us to one another in ways that are profound, that are beautiful, that are true.

The Beauty of Connection: Seeing Ourselves in Each Other

Connection is the essence of relationships, the spark that draws us together, the bridge that allows us to cross into each other's worlds. To connect is to see and to be seen, to hear and to be heard, to know and to be known. It is a dance of empathy, a meeting of hearts, a recognition of our shared humanity.

In connection, we find a happiness that is gentle, a joy that is quiet, a peace that arises from knowing that we are part of something larger, that we are woven into the fabric of life, that we are held in the warmth of human companionship. Connection is a reminder that we are not alone, that we are part of a community, a family, a circle of love. It is the touchstone of happiness, the foundation of well-being, the heart of a life that is rich, that is meaningful, that is full.

To truly connect with another is to open ourselves, to lower our walls, to allow ourselves to be vulnerable. It is to say, "Here I am, in all my beauty, in all my imperfections," and to accept the other with the same love, the same openness, the same compassion. In this openness, we find a joy that is as steady as the breath, as enduring as the heart, as boundless as the soul.

The Power of Empathy: Walking in Another's Shoes

Empathy is the heart of connection, the soul of relationships, the bridge that allows us to understand, to feel, to be with another in their joy and in their sorrow. Empathy is the art of stepping into another's world, of seeing life through their eyes, of feeling with them, of being with them. It is a profound act of love, a gift that we give not only to others but to ourselves.

To practice empathy is to live with an open heart, to listen with intention, to be present with compassion. It is to let go of judgment, to release the need for control, to embrace the other as they are, with all their dreams, all their fears, all their beautiful, messy, human complexity. In empathy, we find a joy that is rooted in understanding, a happiness that arises from connection, a contentment that comes from knowing that we are not alone.

Empathy is the foundation of relationships, the thread that binds us, the glue that holds us together. It is the power to see ourselves in another, to recognize our shared humanity, to know that we are part of a larger whole, a larger love, a larger life.

The Gift of Love: The Heartbeat of Happiness

Love is the heartbeat of relationships, the essence of connection, the soul of life. To love is to give of ourselves freely, without expectation, without condition, without the need for anything in return. It is to open our hearts, to share our lives, to create a bond that is deep, that is meaningful, that is true.

In love, we find a happiness that is pure, a joy that is full, a peace that is complete. Love is not about possession; it is about freedom, about allowing the other to be fully themselves, about celebrating their uniqueness, their beauty, their individuality. In love, we find a joy that is shared, a happiness that is multiplied, a contentment that is boundless.

To love is to see the beauty in another, to honour their journey, to support their growth, to cherish their presence. It is to be with them in their joy, in their sorrow, in their dreams, in their fears. Love is the light that brightens the world, the warmth that heals the heart, the song that fills the soul. In love, we find a happiness that is eternal, a joy that is infinite, a peace that is as vast as the universe.

Nurturing Relationships: Building Bonds That Last

Relationships, like all living things, require care, attention, love. They are not static; they are dynamic, ever-changing, ever-evolving, a dance of connection, a symphony of love. To nurture a relationship is to invest in its growth, to be present, to be patient, to be kind. It is to create a space for love to flourish, for connection to deepen, for happiness to grow.

Nurturing a relationship means listening, truly listening, with an open heart, with a mind that is present, with a soul that is compassionate. It means being there, through the highs and the lows, through the moments of joy and the moments of sorrow. It means honouring the other, supporting them, encouraging them, celebrating them.

When we nurture our relationships, we create bonds that are strong, that are resilient, that are enduring. We create a foundation of love, of trust, of respect. And in this foundation, we find a happiness that is steady, a joy that is full, a peace that is complete.

Stories of Connection: Lives Enriched by Love

Throughout history, there are stories of relationships that have transformed lives, that have uplifted hearts, that have created a legacy of love. These stories remind us of the power of connection, of the beauty of empathy, of the joy of love.

Consider the story of Helen Keller and her teacher, Anne Sullivan. Through patience, compassion, and love, Anne helped Helen break through the darkness of silence and isolation, opening her world to communication, to connection, to understanding. Their relationship was one of mutual respect, profound empathy, and enduring love. Through this bond, Helen found not only knowledge but joy, not only understanding but happiness.

Or think of the friendship between C.S. Lewis and J.R.R. Tolkien, two authors who inspired, challenged, and supported each other in their creative pursuits. Through their relationship, they found a sense of belonging, a camaraderie, a shared joy in their passion for storytelling and truth. Their friendship was a source of strength, a bond of love, a testament to the power of connection.

These stories inspire us to cherish our relationships, to nurture our connections, to live with love, with empathy, with kindness. They remind us that happiness is found not in isolation, but in connection, not in solitude, but in companionship, not in separateness, but in unity.

Practices for Building Emotional Bonds

Building meaningful relationships is a journey, a practice, a way of living that requires intention, presence, and love. Below are practices that can help us nurture our relationships, that can guide us on the path to deeper connections, that can create a life that is rich in love, in joy, in happiness.

1. Practice Active Listening: Listening is the foundation of connection, a way of showing love, of being present, of honouring the other. Practice listening with intention, with empathy, with an open heart. This practice helps to build trust, to foster understanding, to create a bond that is deep, that is true.

2. Express Appreciation: Take time to express gratitude for those in your life, to acknowledge their presence, to celebrate their uniqueness, to honour their contributions. This practice of appreciation helps to strengthen the bond, to deepen the connection, to create a foundation of love.

3. Be Present: Relationships require presence, a willingness to be with the other, to share in their joy, to support them in their sorrow, to live fully in each moment. Practice being present with those you love, offering your full attention, your compassion, your love.

4. Show Vulnerability: Connection is built on honesty, on openness, on vulnerability. Practice being real, being open, being yourself with those you love. This practice helps to create a bond that is authentic, a connection that is deep, a relationship that is fulfilling.

5. Create Shared Experiences: Spend time together, create memories, share experiences, build a life that is woven with love, with laughter, with joy. This practice of shared experiences helps to strengthen the bond, to create a sense of belonging, to build a foundation of happiness.

The Joy of Relationships: A Happiness That is Shared

Relationships are the heart of happiness, the foundation of well-being, the symphony of life. In relationships, we

find a joy that is shared, a love that is multiplied, a happiness that is boundless. For in connection, we discover a sense of belonging, a feeling of being seen, a love that is as deep as the soul.

As we continue this journey, may we carry with us the gift of relationships, the knowledge that we are part of a larger whole, that we are connected to others, that we are held in the embrace of love. May we find in relationships a path to happiness, a source of joy, a way of living that is meaningful, that is rich, that is real.

For in the symphony of relationships, we find the true essence of happiness—a happiness that is not found in solitude, but in connection, a joy that is not about self, but about love, a contentment that is as deep as the bonds we share.

CHAPTER 13: THE WISDOM OF LAUGHTER – FINDING LEVITY AMIDST LIFE'S TRIALS

There is a wisdom in laughter, a lightness that lifts the spirit, a joy that refreshes the soul. Laughter is a balm, a release, a reminder that even amidst life's trials, there is room for joy, for levity, for hope. It is the spark that brightens a dark day, the melody that plays through sorrow, the moment of relief that brings us back to ourselves. Laughter is not an escape from life's challenges; it is a way of embracing them, of softening their edges, of finding resilience through joy.

To laugh is to be present, to let go of worry, to surrender to the moment. It is a reminder that life, even in its complexity, is full of beauty, of humour, of irony. Laughter is the language of the heart, a shared expression of our common humanity, a celebration of our capacity to find light even in the darkest times. In laughter, we find a happiness that is pure, a joy that is free, a peace that reminds us that we are not alone.

In this chapter, we explore laughter as a source of healing, as a tool for resilience, as a gift that elevates the spirit and transforms hardship into hope. For in laughter, we discover a path to happiness that is light, that is bright, that is filled with the wisdom of the heart.

The Healing Power of Laughter: A Gift for Body and Soul

Laughter is more than a fleeting moment of joy; it is a profound force for healing, a natural remedy that soothes the body, the mind, and the soul. When we laugh, our bodies release endorphins—those "feel-good" hormones that reduce pain, relieve stress, and bring a sense of calm and well-being. Laughter strengthens the immune system, lowers blood pressure, improves heart health, and relaxes the muscles. It is a gift to the body, a gentle, natural form of healing that requires no prescription, no effort, no cost.

But the healing power of laughter goes beyond the physical; it touches the heart, the spirit, the soul. In laughter, we release not only tension, but fear, worry, sorrow. We give ourselves permission to be light, to let go, to find joy even in difficult moments. Laughter reconnects us to our inner child, to a state of innocence, of wonder, of pure, unfiltered joy.

Through laughter, we find a resilience that is not about resistance, but about release. It is the power to face life's challenges with a light heart, to see the humour in our own struggles, to laugh at our own fears. Laughter is a reminder that we are not defined by our difficulties, that we are more than our worries, that we are capable of finding joy, even amidst pain.

The Joy of Humour: Finding Levity in Everyday Life

Humour is a lens through which we can view life with lightness, with curiosity, with grace. It is the art of seeing the world not as a burden, but as a source of wonder, of joy, of delight. Humour is not about denying reality; it is about embracing it with a smile, about finding the absurd, the ironic, the unexpected in the everyday. Through humour, we learn to take life a little less seriously, to find joy in the simple, to find beauty in the unexpected.

To live with humour is to cultivate a spirit of playfulness, a heart that is open, a mind that is willing to see life as a dance, a story, a journey. It is to laugh at our own mistakes, to find the humour in our own imperfections, to embrace our own humanity with a light heart. Humour is a gift we give to ourselves, a way of finding joy in the everyday, a reminder that life, even in its challenges, is full of moments of laughter, of lightness, of joy.

Imagine, for a moment, seeing life as a comedy rather than a tragedy, as a dance rather than a struggle, as a series of joyful, unexpected moments. This is the gift of humour—a gift that transforms hardship into hope, worry into wonder, pain into play. Through humour, we find a happiness that is as light as a feather, as free as the wind, as gentle as a smile.

Laughter as Connection: The Bond of Shared Joy

Laughter is a universal language, a bond that connects us, a joy that is shared. When we laugh together, we create a moment of unity, a space of understanding, a feeling of belonging. Laughter breaks down barriers, dissolves differences, builds bridges. It is a reminder that we are not alone, that we are part of a larger whole, that we are connected by our shared humanity.

In laughter, we see ourselves in each other, we recognize our common struggles, our shared joys, our mutual dreams. We realize that, beneath all our differences, we are the same—imperfect, hopeful, human. Laughter creates a bond that is light, that is joyful, that is filled with love. It is a reminder that happiness is not a solitary pursuit, but a shared experience, a gift that grows when it is given, a joy that is multiplied when it is shared.

To laugh with others is to connect, to find joy in companionship, to experience a moment of pure, unfiltered happiness. It is a reminder that we are stronger together, that we are uplifted by each other, that we are enriched by our connections, our relationships, our shared laughter.

Stories of Laughter: Lives Brightened by Humour

Throughout history, there are stories of individuals who have used laughter as a tool for resilience, as a source of joy, as a way of facing life's trials with grace, with courage, with levity. These stories remind us of the power of laughter, of the joy that comes from finding humour in hardship, of the strength that arises from a heart that is light.

Consider the story of Viktor Frankl, a Holocaust survivor who found solace in humour even in the darkest of times. Frankl, who endured unimaginable suffering, discovered that laughter was a way of transcending pain, of finding a sense of freedom, of reclaiming his humanity. He used humour as a tool for survival, a way of finding meaning, a way of holding onto hope. Through his laughter, he found a strength that could not be broken, a joy that could not be taken, a peace that endured.

Or take the story of Robin Williams, a comedian who brought joy to millions through his humour, his wit, his spirit of playfulness. Williams understood the power of laughter, the way it could uplift, heal, connect. His life was a testament to the beauty of humour, a reminder that laughter is not only a gift we give to ourselves, but a gift we give to the world. Through his laughter, he brought light, he brought love, he brought joy.

These stories inspire us to embrace laughter, to live with a light heart, to find joy even in life's trials. They remind us that laughter is not only a way of coping, but a way of living, a way of finding happiness, a way of experiencing life in its fullness.

Practices for Embracing Laughter and Humour

Laughter is a practice, a habit, a way of being that can be cultivated, nurtured, embraced. Below are practices that can help us invite more laughter, more joy, more lightness into our lives, practices that can guide us on the path to a life that is rich in humour, in happiness, in healing.

1. Find Humour in Everyday Moments: Practice seeing the humour in everyday life, in the small, unexpected,

delightful moments. Look for reasons to smile, to laugh, to find joy in the ordinary. This practice helps to cultivate a spirit of playfulness, a heart that is light, a mind that is open.

2. Surround Yourself with Laughter: Spend time with people who make you laugh, who uplift you, who bring joy into your life. Watch a funny movie, read a humorous book, listen to a comedian. This practice helps to create an environment of joy, a space of laughter, a life that is filled with levity.

3. Laugh at Yourself: Practice laughing at your own mistakes, your own imperfections, your own quirks. This practice of self-compassion helps to release tension, to embrace your own humanity, to live with a heart that is open, a spirit that is free.

4. Share Laughter with Others: Invite others to laugh with you, to share in moments of joy, to find humour in life's challenges. This practice helps to build connection, to foster companionship, to create bonds of shared happiness.

5. Reflect on Moments of Joy: At the end of each day, take a moment to reflect on the moments of laughter, of joy, of lightness that filled your day. This reflection helps to reinforce the power of laughter, to remind you of its beauty, to inspire you to live with a heart that is light, a soul that is joyful.

The Joy of Laughter: A Path to Resilience and Happiness

Laughter is a path to resilience, a source of joy, a way of finding happiness through lightness, through levity, through love. It is a happiness that is not burdened by worry, that is not weighed down by fear, that is as free as a bird, as bright as the sun, as pure as the heart.

As we continue this journey, may we carry with us the gift of laughter, the knowledge that we are capable of finding joy, even amidst life's trials, that we are strong enough to face hardship with a light heart, that we are free to laugh, to smile, to find peace.

In laughter, we find a true happiness, a boundless joy, a contentment that is as deep as the love we hold within.

CHAPTER 14: HARNESSING OPTIMISM – THE SCIENCE OF HOPE

There is a quiet power in optimism, a light that shines even in the shadows, a vision that sees beyond obstacles to possibilities, beyond endings to new beginnings. Optimism is more than wishful thinking; it is a practiced skill, a mindset that transforms our view of the world, a science-backed approach that fuels resilience, joy, and hope. To live with optimism is to believe in the potential for good, to trust in the unfolding of life, to approach each day with a heart that is open, a mind that is curious, a soul that is brave.

Optimism is not blind to life's struggles; it does not deny pain, nor does it ignore hardship. Instead, optimism is the choice to see beauty in the midst of difficulty, to find strength in the face of adversity, to hold onto hope even when the path is uncertain. It is the art of looking at life through a lens of possibility, a belief that challenges can be stepping stones, that setbacks can be teachers, that every moment holds within it a seed of growth, of wisdom, of joy.

In this chapter, we delve into the science of optimism, exploring how a hopeful outlook can be cultivated, nurtured, strengthened. For in optimism, we find a happiness that is steady, a resilience that is strong, a hope that reminds us that no matter what we face, there is always a way forward, always a reason to believe, always a reason to hope.

The Science of Optimism: A Pathway to Resilience

Optimism is not a fleeting emotion; it is a mindset rooted in science, a perspective that has been shown to enhance resilience, reduce stress, and increase happiness. Research in positive psychology reveals that optimists are more likely to experience better health, greater life satisfaction, and a stronger sense of purpose. They are not immune to life's difficulties, but they face them with a spirit of determination, a belief that challenges can be overcome, that adversity can be a catalyst for growth.

At the heart of optimism is the concept of "cognitive reframing," the ability to interpret events in a positive light, to focus not on what is lost but on what is possible, to see setbacks not as endings but as beginnings. This practice of reframing allows us to shift our perspective, to choose thoughts that empower us, to cultivate a mindset that is focused on solutions, on possibilities, on hope.

Optimism is not only a mental skill; it is a practice that reshapes the brain, that strengthens neural pathways associated with positivity, resilience, and well-being. Studies show that when we engage in optimistic thinking, our brains release dopamine—a "feel-good" chemical that enhances motivation, that lifts our spirits, that fuels our sense of joy. Optimism is a science-backed approach to happiness, a way of building resilience, a skill that can be learned, that can be strengthened, that can transform the way we experience life.

Seeing Possibilities: A Mindset of Opportunity

To live with optimism is to see the world as a canvas of possibilities, to believe that each moment holds within it the potential for something beautiful, something meaningful, something new. Optimism is the art of looking at life with curiosity, of finding opportunity in the unexpected, of embracing change with a heart that is hopeful, a mind that is open, a spirit that is adventurous.

Imagine, for a moment, approaching each day with a sense of possibility, seeing challenges not as barriers but as opportunities, viewing difficulties not as setbacks but as stepping stones. This is the gift of optimism—a mindset that allows us to dream, to imagine, to believe in our own capacity to create, to grow, to transform. Optimism is not about denying reality; it is about seeing reality through a lens of hope, a perspective that is focused on what can be, on what is yet to come, on the potential that lies within each experience.

Through optimism, we learn to embrace the unknown, to trust in the journey, to find joy in the unfolding of life. We become not only resilient but resourceful, not only hopeful but courageous, not only joyful but grateful. In seeing possibilities, we create a life that is filled with meaning, with purpose, with hope.

The Power of Hope: A Beacon in Times of Darkness

Hope is the heart of optimism, the light that guides us through difficult times, the force that propels us forward when all else seems uncertain. To live with hope is to believe that there is always a way, that there is always a reason to keep going, that even in the darkest night, there is a star, a glimmer, a promise of dawn. Hope is not a passive feeling; it is an active choice, a commitment to face life with courage, to embrace each moment with trust, to hold onto the belief that tomorrow holds something good.

Hope does not deny pain; it does not erase struggle. Instead, hope is the strength to carry on, the resilience to rise again, the faith to believe in the possibility of renewal, of healing, of joy. Hope is the force that sustains us, that lifts us, that reminds us that we are capable of enduring, of growing, of finding light even in the darkest of places.

To cultivate hope is to practice gratitude, to focus on the good, to surround ourselves with positivity, with inspiration, with love. It is to hold onto the vision of what is possible, to trust in our own strength, to believe in the beauty of life, even when it is hidden, even when it is hard to see. For in hope, we find a happiness that is steady, a joy that is unwavering, a peace that is profound.

Stories of Optimism: Lives Guided by Hope

Throughout history, there are stories of individuals who have faced unimaginable challenges, yet found the strength to endure, the courage to hope, the resilience to rise. These stories remind us of the power of optimism, of the joy that comes from believing in possibilities, of the strength that arises from a heart that is hopeful, a soul that is brave.

Consider the story of Helen Keller, who lost her sight and hearing at a young age, yet lived a life filled with purpose, with joy, with meaning. Through optimism, she found a way to communicate, to connect, to inspire. Her life was a testament to the power of hope, a reminder that we are capable of transcending even the greatest of limitations, that we are capable of creating a life that is rich, that is beautiful, that is full.

Or take the story of Nelson Mandela, who endured 27 years of imprisonment yet emerged with a spirit that was unbroken, a heart that was filled with forgiveness, a vision that was guided by hope. His optimism was not a denial of the harsh realities he faced; it was a strength that allowed him to endure, to heal, to create a legacy of peace, of justice, of love. Through his hope, he changed the world, inspiring millions, creating a future that was brighter, more just, more beautiful.

These stories inspire us to live with optimism, to believe in our own strength, to find hope even in times of darkness. They remind us that optimism is not only a way of thinking but a way of living, a way of being, a way of experiencing life with courage, with joy, with love.

Practices for Cultivating Optimism and Hope

Optimism is a practice, a habit, a way of being that can be cultivated, nurtured, strengthened. Below are practices that can help us embrace optimism, that can guide us on the path to a life filled with hope, with joy, with resilience.

1. Practice Gratitude: Focus on the good in each day, on

the moments of joy, on the blessings, on the beauty. Write down three things you are grateful for each day. This practice helps to shift your focus, to create a mindset of positivity, to nurture a spirit of optimism.

2. Reframe Challenges: When faced with a difficulty, practice reframing it as an opportunity for growth, as a chance to learn, as a stepping stone on your journey. This practice of cognitive reframing helps to cultivate a mindset of resilience, to see challenges as opportunities, to find strength in adversity.

3. Visualize Positive Outcomes: Take time to visualize your dreams, your goals, your vision for the future. Imagine yourself succeeding, thriving, living a life that is filled with joy, with purpose, with fulfilment. This practice helps to create a sense of possibility, a belief in your own potential, a foundation of hope.

4. Surround Yourself with Positivity: Spend time with people who uplift you, who inspire you, who believe in you. Surround yourself with positivity, with love, with encouragement. This practice helps to create an environment that fosters optimism, that nurtures hope, that supports your journey.

5. Set Small, Achievable Goals: Break down your goals into small, manageable steps, and celebrate each success along the way. This practice of setting and achieving goals helps to build confidence, to create a sense of progress, to foster a spirit of optimism.

The Joy of Optimism: A Life Filled with Hope

Optimism is a pathway to joy, a source of resilience, a way of finding happiness through hope, through belief, through love. It is a happiness that is not dependent on circumstance, but on perspective, a joy that is not bound by what is, but by what can be, a contentment

that is rooted in the knowledge that we are capable, that we are strong, that we are filled with potential.

As we continue this journey, may we carry with us the gift of optimism, the knowledge that we are capable of creating a life that is filled with joy, with meaning, with love. May we find in optimism a pathway to happiness, a source of strength, a way of living that is light, that is bright, that is filled with hope.

In optimism, we find a happiness that is deep, a joy that is steady, a peace that is as boundless as the love we hold within.

CHAPTER 15: COURAGE TO CHANGE – EMBRACING GROWTH AND TRANSFORMATION

Change is the heartbeat of life, a quiet force that pulses through every moment, whispering to us to move forward, to evolve, to grow. It is the gentle tide that shifts us from the shores of familiarity, urging us to explore, to let go, to become. In change, we are invited to shed the past, to step into the new, to trust that even when we feel most vulnerable, we are on a path toward something greater, something truer, something deeply meaningful.

But change requires courage. It asks us to surrender our comfort, to brave the unknown, to face parts of ourselves that may have remained hidden, unexplored, unchallenged. To change is to dance with uncertainty, to embrace a process of transformation that is both beautiful and unsettling. And yet, it is in this journey that we find a happiness that is resilient, a joy that is profound, a sense of fulfilment that is as expansive as the horizon.

In this chapter, we explore change not as a disruption, but as a dance of growth, a transformative journey that leads us to the heart of who we are. For in the courage to change, we discover a happiness that is rooted not in staying the same, but in evolving, in becoming, in continually shaping ourselves into the person we were meant to be.

The Essence of Transformation: Unfolding Into Who We Are

Transformation is the soul's journey of unfolding, a path that takes us inward and outward, allowing us to grow into our true essence. It is a process of letting go of the masks we wear, the roles we cling to, the beliefs that no longer serve us. Transformation is not about changing into someone else; it is about becoming more fully ourselves, about aligning our lives with our deepest values, about letting our true selves shine through.

Imagine a caterpillar that enters its cocoon, surrendering to the darkness, to the unknown, to the alchemy of transformation. It does not resist; it does not cling to what it was. Instead, it lets go, trusting in the process, embracing the journey of becoming. And when it emerges, it is no longer the same—it has become a butterfly, a creature of beauty, of grace, of freedom. This is the essence of transformation—a journey of unfolding, a process of becoming, a path that leads us to the wings we never knew we had.

To embrace transformation is to trust in this process of becoming, to believe in our own potential, to know that we are capable of growing, of evolving, of becoming more than we ever dreamed possible. It is to live with a sense of wonder, a curiosity, a willingness to be shaped by life's experiences, to allow each moment to bring us closer to the fullness of who we are. For in transformation, we find a happiness that is deep, a joy that is true, a life that is rich, that is meaningful, that is full.

The Courage to Change: Stepping Beyond the Familiar

Change is a journey that requires courage—a willingness to leave behind the familiar, to venture into the unknown, to embrace the uncertainty that comes with growth. It is an act of bravery, a leap of faith, a commitment to living a life that is dynamic, that is expansive, that is true. The courage to change is not about eliminating fear; it is about moving forward despite it, about trusting in our own strength, about believing that we are capable of facing whatever lies ahead.

To step beyond the familiar is to open ourselves to new experiences, to new perspectives, to new possibilities. It is to release the safety of what we know, to surrender to the mystery of what we do not. This is not an easy path, but it is one that brings us closer to the essence of who we are, that fills our lives with meaning, with purpose, with joy.

Courage is the foundation of change, the strength that allows us to take that first step, to face our fears, to embrace the journey of growth. And in this courage, we find a happiness that is resilient, a joy that is steady, a peace that arises from knowing that we are on the path of becoming, that we are living in alignment with our highest potential.

Growth as a Journey of Discovery: A Path to Inner Joy

Growth is not a destination; it is a journey, a process of continual discovery, a path that leads us deeper into the heart of life. To grow is to be willing to learn, to be open to change, to embrace each experience as a stepping stone on our path. Growth is the process of expanding our horizons, of breaking through our limitations, of becoming more of who we truly are.

In growth, we find a joy that is rooted not in achievement, but in evolution, not in what we gain, but in who we become. Growth is the joy of seeing ourselves transform, of witnessing our own resilience, of realizing that we are capable of more than we ever thought possible. It is a happiness that is not tied to success or failure, but to the journey itself, to the act of becoming, to the beauty of unfolding.

Imagine a river that flows through mountains, carving its path through rock and earth, finding its way to the sea. It does not stay in one place; it is constantly moving, constantly changing, constantly becoming. And in this movement, it finds its joy, its purpose, its fulfilment. Growth is like this river—a journey of discovery, a path of becoming, a process that leads us to a life that is rich, that is full, that is deeply, profoundly joyful.

The Role of Change in Happiness: Embracing Life's Fluidity

Happiness is not found in staying the same; it is found in embracing change, in living with a heart that is open to life's flow, in being willing to evolve. Change is not a disruption of happiness; it is an essential part of it. For happiness is a dynamic state, a journey of growth, a process of transformation. To be truly happy is to be open to life's fluidity, to embrace the cycles of change, to celebrate each moment of becoming.

When we resist change, we limit ourselves, we confine our lives to the narrow borders of comfort, we hold ourselves back from the fullness of who we are meant to be. But when we embrace change, we open ourselves to a life that is vibrant, that is expansive, that is filled with possibility. Change is the path to happiness, a reminder that we are not meant to stay the same, but to evolve, to grow, to live a life that is as dynamic as the universe itself.

To see change as an essential component of happiness is to understand that life is not a fixed state, but a flowing river, a dance, a journey. It is to live with a sense of wonder, a willingness to be shaped by each experience, a joy in the unfolding of our own becoming. For in change, we find a happiness that is not tied to what is, but to what can be, a joy that is as boundless as the sky, a peace that is as deep as the soul.

Stories of Transformation: Lives Illuminated by Growth

Throughout time, there have been countless individuals who have embraced change, who have found joy in transformation, who have lived lives that were illuminated by growth, by courage, by resilience. These stories remind us of the beauty of change, of the happiness that comes from becoming, of the strength that arises from a heart that is willing to evolve.

Consider the story of Nelson Mandela, a man who endured decades of imprisonment, yet emerged with a spirit that was unbroken, a heart that was filled with forgiveness, a vision that was guided by hope. Mandela's journey of transformation was not an easy one, but it was one that led him to a life of purpose, of impact, of joy. Through his courage to change, he found a path that was aligned with his values, his dreams, his highest aspirations.

Or think of Maya Angelou, who transformed her life from one of silence and hardship to one of expression and empowerment. Through her journey of growth, Angelou found a voice that spoke not only for herself, but for others, a voice that inspired, that uplifted, that healed. Her life was a testament to the power of transformation, a reminder that we are capable of creating lives that are meaningful, that are fulfilling, that are rich with joy.

These stories inspire us to embrace change, to live with courage, to see our own lives as a journey of growth. They remind us that transformation is not only possible, but beautiful, that happiness is not only a state of being, but a process of becoming, a journey that leads us closer to our own potential.

Practices for Embracing Change and Fostering Transformation

Change and growth are practices, habits, ways of living that require intention, courage, and a willingness to evolve. Below are practices that can help us embrace change, that can guide us on the path to growth, that can create a life that is rich in happiness, in meaning, in fulfilment.

1. Set Clear Intentions for Growth: Reflect on your goals, your dreams, your vision for who you want to become. Set clear intentions for your growth, for your transformation, for your journey of becoming. This practice helps to create a sense of direction, to align your actions with your values, to foster a spirit of growth.

2. Embrace Challenges as Teachers: Practice viewing challenges as opportunities for growth, as moments that can teach you, that can shape you, that can guide you. This perspective helps to create a mindset of resilience, to see obstacles as teachers, to find wisdom in adversity.

3. Celebrate Small Changes: Take time to acknowledge the small changes, the subtle shifts, the moments of growth that may go unnoticed. Celebrate these small steps, honour your journey, recognize your progress. This practice of celebration helps to create a sense of fulfilment, a joy in the process of becoming, a happiness that is rooted in the journey.

4. Surround Yourself with Encouragement: Spend time with people who believe in your potential, who support your growth, who inspire your transformation. Surround yourself with positivity, with love, with encouragement. This practice helps to create an environment that nurtures growth, that supports courage, that fosters joy.

5. Practice Patience and Self-Compassion: Change is a journey that takes time, that requires patience, that calls for kindness. Be gentle with yourself, be patient with your progress, be compassionate with your journey. This practice of self-compassion helps to create a space of

peace, a foundation of love, a heart that is open to growth.

The Joy of Transformation: A Life That is Full

Transformation is a journey to happiness, a path to joy, a way of finding fulfilment through growth, through change, through becoming. It is a happiness that is not bound by what we have, but by who we are, a joy that is rooted not in staying the same, but in evolving, a contentment that arises from knowing that we are living a life that is rich, that is full, that is true.

As we continue this journey, may we carry with us the courage to change, the strength to grow, the belief that we are capable of transforming our lives in ways that are beautiful, that are profound, that are true. May we find in transformation a path to happiness, a source of strength, a way of living that is vibrant, that is expansive, that is filled with hope.

Within the courage to change, we find a happiness that is deep, a joy that is steady, a peace that is as boundless as the love we hold within.

CHAPTER 16: THE ART OF LETTING GO – FINDING FREEDOM IN RELEASE

To let go is to unlock the chains that bind us, to release the weights we carry, to step into a life that is light, free, unburdened. Letting go is not about forgetting; it is about freeing ourselves from the grip of the past, from the hold of regret, from the clutches of worry. It is a journey of softening, of surrendering, of allowing ourselves to move forward with grace, with peace, with hope.

The art of letting go is a practice of the heart, a gentle release of all that no longer serves us. It is a conscious choice to unbind ourselves from the stories that no longer define us, from the grudges that only wound us, from the worries that cloud our present. In letting go, we find not only peace but a joy that is quiet, a freedom that is profound, a happiness that is as light as the breath, as gentle as the breeze.

In this chapter, we explore the beauty of letting go, the freedom that arises from release, the peace that comes from surrender. For in letting go, we discover a happiness that is steady, a contentment that is unwavering, a life that is open, spacious, and full of possibility.

The Weight of Holding On: Grudges, Regrets, and Worries

We often hold onto memories, to moments, to feelings that weigh us down, that tether us to the past, that keep us from experiencing the fullness of the present. We carry grudges like stones in our pockets, regrets like shadows on our hearts, worries like clouds in our minds. These burdens may seem small, but they accumulate, they grow heavy, they drain us of energy, of joy, of peace.

To hold onto a grudge is to keep a wound open, to allow bitterness to take root, to build walls around our hearts. Grudges do not protect us; they imprison us. They keep us trapped in anger, in resentment, in pain. When we let go of a grudge, we release ourselves, we free our hearts, we make room for compassion, for understanding, for love.

Regret, too, is a weight we often carry—a sorrow for what could have been, a longing for a different outcome, a wish for another chance. But regret ties us to the past, it blinds us to the present, it holds us back from the life that is waiting to unfold. To let go of regret is to accept what is, to honour the lessons of the past, to forgive ourselves, to find peace in the knowledge that we did the best we could.

Worry is a thief of joy, a shadow that clouds the mind, a fear that paralyzes the heart. When we worry, we create stories of what could go wrong, we imagine worst-case scenarios, we live in a future that may never come. But worry does not protect us; it only robs us of the present. To let go of worry is to trust in life, to believe in our own resilience, to have faith that we can face whatever comes our way.

The Freedom of Release: A Path to Inner Peace

To release is to unburden, to let go, to create space within. It is an act of compassion, a gift we give to ourselves, a doorway to freedom, to peace, to joy. When we let go, we do not lose; we gain. We gain a lightness of spirit, a clarity of mind, a heart that is open, a life that is free.

Imagine, for a moment, a balloon filled with helium, tied to the ground by a string. It yearns to rise, to soar, to be free. But it is held down, tethered, unable to reach its full height. When we cut the string, the balloon floats upward, released from its burden, free to explore the vastness of the sky. In the same way, when we let go of what binds us, we free ourselves to rise, to expand, to experience life with a heart that is light, a mind that is clear, a soul that is unbound.

The freedom of release is a joy that comes from within, a happiness that is not dependent on circumstance, a peace that is as steady as the breath. When we let go, we find a freedom that is not about escape, but about acceptance, a joy that is not about absence, but about presence, a contentment that is rooted in trust, in surrender, in love.

Letting Go of Grudges: The Power of Forgiveness

Forgiveness is the art of releasing the past, of letting go of the pain, of finding peace within. To forgive is not to condone; it is to release ourselves from the weight of anger, from the burden of resentment, from the prison of bitterness. Forgiveness is a gift we give to ourselves, a doorway to freedom, a path to healing.

When we forgive, we open our hearts, we create space for compassion, for empathy, for understanding. We let go of the need to be right, of the desire for revenge, of the weight of the past. In forgiveness, we find a joy that is gentle, a peace that is profound, a freedom that is true.

To forgive is to let go of the story that binds us, to release the hurt that wounds us, to open ourselves to the possibility of love, of healing, of peace. In forgiveness, we find not only freedom but a happiness that is deep, a joy that is steady, a contentment that is as vast as the soul.

Releasing Regret: Embracing Acceptance

Regret is a longing for what could have been, a sorrow for what was lost, a wish for a different outcome. But regret keeps us tied to the past, it holds us back from the life that is unfolding, it blinds us to the beauty of the present. To let go of regret is to accept what is, to honour the lessons of the past, to find peace in the knowledge that each moment is a part of our journey.

When we release regret, we free ourselves from the grip of "if only," we open ourselves to the possibility of now, we embrace the life that is here, that is real, that is true. Letting go of regret is an act of self-compassion, a choice to be kind to ourselves, to forgive our mistakes, to trust in our own growth, in our own journey.

In releasing regret, we find a happiness that is rooted in acceptance, a joy that arises from presence, a peace that is as gentle as a sigh. For in letting go of the past, we make room for the present, for the beauty of the moment, for the fullness of life.

Surrendering Worry: Trusting in Life's Flow

Worry is a shadow that clouds the mind, a fear that holds us back, a burden that weighs us down. When we worry, we live in a future that may never come, we create stories of what could go wrong, we rob ourselves of the joy of the present. But worry does not protect us; it only drains us, it limits us, it keeps us from experiencing the fullness of life.

To let go of worry is to trust in life, to believe in our own resilience, to have faith that we are capable of facing whatever comes our way. It is a choice to live with a heart that is open, a mind that is clear, a spirit that is free. In surrendering worry, we find a freedom that is light, a joy that is true, a peace that is steady.

To release worry is to embrace the present, to trust in the journey, to live with a sense of wonder, of curiosity, of joy. In this freedom, we find a happiness that is not dependent on control, but on acceptance, a contentment that arises from trust, from surrender, from love.

Practices for Letting Go and Finding Freedom

Letting go is a practice, a habit, a way of being that requires intention, presence, and love. Below are practices that can help us embrace the art of letting go, that can guide us on the path to freedom, that can create a life that is rich in peace, in joy, in fulfilment.

1. Practice Forgiveness: Take time to reflect on any grudges, any resentments, any anger you may be holding onto. Practice forgiveness, not as a gift to others, but as

a gift to yourself, a way of freeing your heart, of opening yourself to peace, to love.

2. Release Regret through Gratitude: Reflect on the past, on the lessons learned, on the growth experienced. Practice gratitude for each moment, each experience, each lesson. This practice helps to transform regret into acceptance, to create a sense of peace, to embrace the beauty of the journey.

3. Surrender Worry through Mindfulness: Practice mindfulness, focusing on the present moment, on the breath, on the sensations of the body. This practice helps to release worry, to create a sense of grounding, to find peace in the here and now.

4. Visualize Freedom: Take time to visualize yourself letting go, releasing each burden, each weight, each worry. Imagine yourself as light, as free, as open. This visualization helps to create a sense of freedom, to inspire a spirit of release, to foster a heart that is unbound.

5. Create a Letting Go Ritual: Practice a simple ritual of release, whether it is writing down your worries and burning them, or visualizing them floating away like leaves on a river. This ritual helps to create a sense of closure, to symbolize the act of letting go, to find peace in the process of release.

The Joy of Release: A Life That is Free

Letting go is a path to happiness, a source of peace, a way of finding freedom through release, through surrender, through love. It is a happiness that is not bound by the past, but by the present, a joy that is rooted not in control, but in trust, a contentment that arises from the knowledge that we are free to live, to love, to be.

As we continue this journey, may we carry with us the gift of letting go, the knowledge that we are capable of releasing the past, of embracing the present, of creating a life that is light, that is free, that is full.

Through the art of letting go, we find a happiness that is deep, a joy that is steady, and a peace that is as boundless as the sky.

CHAPTER 18:
THE BALANCE OF SOLITUDE AND CONNECTION – HARMONY IN RELATIONSHIPS

In the symphony of life, solitude and connection are like the quiet notes and the crescendos, each essential to the melody of our existence. Solitude is the sanctuary where we meet ourselves, a place of reflection, of peace, of inner growth. Connection, on the other hand, is the bridge that binds us to others, a path of shared joy, of empathy, of love. Together, solitude and connection create a harmony that nourishes the soul, that enriches the spirit, that brings us closer to happiness.

To live in balance is to honour both our need for solitude and our desire for connection, to find a rhythm that allows us to feel whole, fulfilled, complete. In solitude, we discover our inner world, we listen to the whispers of our heart, we nurture our inner peace. In connection, we share in the joys and sorrows of others, we feel the warmth of companionship, we experience the beauty of intimacy. Both are vital, both are beautiful, both are pathways to joy.

In this chapter, we explore the delicate balance between solitude and connection, the ways in which both contribute to happiness, the harmony that arises when we embrace both as essential elements of a life well-lived. For in this balance, we find a happiness that is rooted not only in self-discovery but in shared experiences, a joy that is as profound as the silence of solitude and as radiant as the warmth of connection.

The Sanctuary of Solitude: Finding Peace Within

Solitude is the art of being alone without loneliness, a place where we retreat not to escape the world, but to meet ourselves, to embrace our own company, to explore the vast landscape of our inner being. In solitude, we find a sanctuary of peace, a place of reflection, a space where we can listen to the quiet voice of our own heart. It is here, in the stillness of solitude, that we come to know ourselves more deeply, to understand our own needs, our own dreams, our own truths.

Imagine the tranquillity of a morning spent alone, the quiet of a forest, the gentle hush of dawn. In these moments, we feel a sense of grounding, a connection to something greater, a peace that arises not from distraction, but from presence. Solitude is not an emptiness; it is a fullness, a richness, a wholeness. It is a time to recharge, to reflect, to find clarity. In solitude, we find not isolation, but intimacy—a closeness with ourselves, a space to honour our own thoughts, our own feelings, our own journey.

To embrace solitude is to nurture our own well-being, to give ourselves permission to be alone, to find comfort in our own presence. Solitude allows us to recharge, to restore, to reconnect with ourselves. And in this reconnection, we find a joy that is quiet, a happiness that is gentle, a peace that is as steady as the breath.

The Beauty of Connection: The Joy of Shared Experiences

Connection is the bridge that links us to others, the thread that weaves us into the fabric of community, the light that brightens our days. To connect is to open our hearts, to share in the joys and sorrows of another, to experience the warmth of companionship, the beauty of friendship, the intimacy of love. Connection is a source of happiness that is profound, a joy that is magnified, a fulfilment that arises from the shared experience of life.

In connection, we find a sense of belonging, a feeling of being seen, understood, cherished. Through connection, we realize that we are not alone, that we are part of a larger whole, that we are held in the embrace of love. Connection is not about losing ourselves in others; it is about finding ourselves in the presence of others, about experiencing life with a heart that is open, a spirit that is compassionate, a soul that is kind.

Imagine the joy of laughter shared with a friend, the comfort of a hug, the warmth of a smile. In these moments, we feel a happiness that is expansive, a joy that is shared, a love that is infinite. Connection reminds us that life is not a solitary journey, but a shared adventure, a dance of love, of friendship, of companionship.

To embrace connection is to open ourselves to the beauty of relationships, to allow others into our lives, to experience the richness of human companionship. Connection allows us to feel supported, uplifted, loved. And in this support, we find a joy that is radiant, a happiness that is boundless, a contentment that is as deep as the heart.

The Dance Between Solitude and Connection: A Harmony of Opposites

The balance between solitude and connection is a dance, a rhythm, a harmony that requires intention, awareness, and love. Too much solitude can lead to isolation, to loneliness, to a sense of disconnection. Too much connection can lead to overwhelm, to a loss of self, to a feeling of being unmoored. But when we find the balance, we create a life that is whole, a happiness that is steady, a peace that is profound.

To find harmony is to honour both our need for solitude and our desire for connection, to create a rhythm that allows us to feel both grounded and uplifted, both complete within ourselves and connected to others. In solitude, we gather strength, we reflect, we recharge. In connection, we share, we give, we experience. Both are necessary, both are beautiful, both are essential to a life that is rich, that is full, that is deeply fulfilling.

Imagine a tree that stands alone in a field, its roots deep, its branches reaching toward the sky. It is strong, it is steady, it is rooted. And yet, it is also part of a forest, surrounded by other trees, connected by the earth, by the air, by the light. In the same way, we are both individuals and part of a community, both solitary and connected, both independent and interdependent.

The Gifts of Solitude and Connection: A Life of Wholeness

Solitude and connection each bring unique gifts, each contribute to our well-being, each nourish our happiness in different ways. Solitude gives us the gift of self-reflection, of inner peace, of a deeper understanding of who we are. It allows us to cultivate a sense of self, to nurture our inner world, to find joy in our own presence.

Connection, on the other hand, gives us the gift of companionship, of shared experiences, of love. It allows us to feel supported, to experience the beauty of friendship, to find joy in the presence of others. Connection reminds us that we are not alone, that we are part of a larger whole, that we are held in the embrace of love.

When we embrace both solitude and connection, we create a life that is whole, a happiness that is balanced, a peace that is profound. We find a joy that is both quiet and expansive, a contentment that is both grounded and uplifting, a life that is both rooted in self-awareness and enriched by relationships.

Practices for Balancing Solitude and Connection

Balancing solitude and connection is a practice, a way of living that requires intention, awareness, and love. Below are practices that can help us embrace both solitude and connection, that can guide us on the path to a life that is rich in harmony, in joy, in happiness.

1. Create a Daily Solitude Practice: Take time each day to be alone, to sit in silence, to reflect, to reconnect with yourself. This practice of solitude helps to nurture your inner world, to cultivate a sense of peace, to find joy in your own presence.

2. Engage in Deep, Meaningful Connections: Spend time with those who uplift you, who inspire you, who support your growth. Engage in conversations that are deep, that are meaningful, that allow you to share and to listen. This practice of connection helps to create a sense of belonging, to foster relationships that are enriching, that are fulfilling.

3. Set Boundaries to Honour Both Needs: Practice setting boundaries that allow you to honour both your need for solitude and your desire for connection. Give yourself permission to say no when you need time alone, and to reach out when you crave companionship. This balance helps to create a life that is both peaceful and vibrant, both introspective and connected.

4. Practice Mindful Presence in Both Solitude and Connection: Whether you are alone or with others, practice being fully present, fully engaged, fully aware. This practice of mindfulness helps to deepen your experience of both solitude and connection, to create a sense of grounding, to foster a life that is rich in meaning, in joy, in love.

5. Reflect on the Gifts of Both Solitude and Connection: Take time to reflect on the ways in which solitude and connection contribute to your happiness, on the unique gifts that each brings to your life. This reflection helps

to create a sense of gratitude, to inspire a life that is balanced, that is harmonious, that is whole.

The Harmony of Solitude and Connection: A Life of Balance

The balance between solitude and connection is a path to happiness, a source of peace, a way of finding harmony through the dance of opposites. It is a happiness that arises not from choosing one over the other, but from embracing both as essential, from finding a rhythm that allows us to feel whole, to feel fulfilled, to feel complete.

As we continue this journey, may we carry with us the wisdom of solitude and the warmth of connection, the knowledge that we are both individuals and part of a larger whole, both unique and united, both solitary and connected. May we find in this balance a pathway to happiness, a source of joy, a way of living that is rich, that is full, that is true.

For in the harmony of solitude and connection, we find a happiness that is deep, a joy that is steady, a peace that is as boundless as the love we hold within.

CHAPTER 19: A JOURNEY THROUGH MINDFULNESS – THE POWER OF PRESENT AWARENESS

Mindfulness is the art of being fully alive, a practice of connecting with the world around us, of immersing ourselves in the beauty of each passing moment. It is an invitation to slow down, to breathe, to notice, to experience life with an open heart, an attentive mind, a spirit that is present. Through mindfulness, we awaken to the richness of existence, to the simple, profound beauty that lies hidden in the ordinary, waiting to be seen, felt, and cherished.

To be mindful is to be rooted in the now, to let go of the

past, to release the future, to embrace the present with a sense of wonder, of gratitude, of joy. It is to live with a heart that is open, a mind that is clear, a soul that is attuned to the subtle symphony of life. In mindfulness, we find a happiness that is quiet, a peace that is deep, a freedom that arises from simply being.

In this chapter, we explore mindfulness as a journey into the present moment, a path that leads us to a heightened sensitivity to life, to an awareness that transforms even the smallest details into sources of joy. For in mindfulness, we discover a happiness that is as steady as the breath, a joy that is as gentle as a breeze, a contentment that is as profound as the silence of dawn.

The Essence of Mindfulness: Awakening to the Present

Mindfulness is the art of presence, a way of being that is fully engaged, fully alive, fully aware. It is not about escaping reality; it is about embracing it, about experiencing life with a depth, a clarity, a sense of wonder. When we are mindful, we open ourselves to the richness of each moment, we become sensitive to the beauty that surrounds us, we discover a joy that is hidden in the ordinary, a peace that lies within.

Imagine, for a moment, standing by a river, watching the water flow, listening to its gentle rhythm, feeling the coolness of the breeze, seeing the sunlight dance on the surface. In this moment, you are not thinking of the past, you are not worrying about the future; you are simply here, fully present, fully alive. This is mindfulness —a practice of surrender, a state of awareness, a way of connecting with the world in its purest form.

To be mindful is to see with fresh eyes, to experience life as if for the first time, to notice the details, the colours, the textures, the sounds. It is a way of grounding ourselves in the here and now, a way of finding beauty in the simple, of discovering joy in the ordinary, of experiencing life in its fullness.

The Practice of Breath Awareness: The Anchor of Presence

The breath is our anchor to the present, a rhythm that connects us to life, a reminder that each moment is a gift. Through breath awareness, we find a way to centre ourselves, to calm the mind, to return to the here and now. The breath is always with us, a constant companion, a gentle reminder that we are alive, that we are here, that we are enough.

To practice breath awareness is to focus on each inhale, each exhale, to feel the sensation of air filling the lungs, to notice the release, the pause, the flow. It is a practice of simplicity, a way of returning to the body, of grounding ourselves in the present. In the breath, we find a source of peace, a sense of calm, a doorway to mindfulness.

Imagine sitting quietly, closing your eyes, feeling the gentle rise and fall of your chest, the steady rhythm of your breath. With each inhale, you bring yourself closer to the present, with each exhale, you release the past, the future, the distractions. In this rhythm, you find a peace that is steady, a joy that is quiet, a presence that is pure. Breath awareness is a pathway to mindfulness, a practice that brings us back to ourselves, that anchors us in the now, that fills our lives with a sense of serenity.

Cultivating Sensory Awareness: Heightening Our Sensitivity to Beauty

Mindfulness is a journey of the senses, an awakening to the beauty that surrounds us, a practice of noticing the details, the subtleties, the nuances of life. To be mindful is to see with fresh eyes, to hear with open ears, to touch with gentle hands, to taste with gratitude, to smell with appreciation. It is to immerse ourselves fully in each experience, to savour each sensation, to experience life in its vivid, radiant, textured fullness.

Imagine the joy of tasting a ripe strawberry, the sweetness, the burst of flavour, the way it fills your senses, your mind, your heart. Imagine the beauty of listening to a piece of music, the way each note resonates, the way the melody unfolds, the way it moves you, touches you, lifts you. Imagine the peace of feeling the warmth of the sun on your skin, the coolness of a breeze, the softness of grass beneath your feet. In these moments, we are fully alive, fully present, fully connected.

To cultivate sensory awareness is to embrace life with a spirit of curiosity, to experience each moment as a gift, to find beauty in the smallest details, the simplest pleasures, the quietest moments. It is a way of grounding ourselves in the present, of opening ourselves to the richness of life, of finding joy in the ordinary, peace in the present, happiness in the now.

Letting Go of Judgment: Embracing Life as It Is

Mindfulness is not about changing the world; it is about embracing it, about experiencing life without judgment, without resistance, without the need to control. To be mindful is to accept each moment as it is, to let go of the labels, the expectations, the judgments that cloud our perception. It is a practice of surrender, a way of finding peace in acceptance, a way of experiencing life with an open heart, a clear mind, a free spirit.

When we let go of judgment, we open ourselves to the beauty of what is, we experience life in its purity, we find joy in the simplicity of being. Imagine walking in nature, noticing the colours of the leaves, the songs of the birds, the scent of the earth. In this moment, you are not judging, you are not analysing, you are simply experiencing. This is mindfulness—a way of being that is open, that is receptive, that is free.

To let go of judgment is to embrace life with compassion, to accept ourselves with kindness, to see the world with clarity, with love, with joy. In this acceptance, we find a happiness that is gentle, a peace that is steady, a contentment that is as vast as the sky.

The Beauty of Stillness: Finding Peace in the Pause

In a world that is constantly moving, mindfulness invites us to pause, to be still, to experience the beauty of silence, the peace of stillness, the joy of simply being. To be mindful is to slow down, to breathe, to savour each moment, to find richness in the pause. Stillness is not emptiness; it is fullness, a quiet presence, a deep peace.

Imagine sitting by a lake, watching the water, feeling the stillness, the calm, the serenity. In this moment, you are not rushing, you are not striving, you are simply here, fully present, fully alive. This is the gift of mindfulness

—a practice that allows us to experience the fullness of life, to find peace in the pause, to embrace the beauty of stillness.

In stillness, we find a joy that is quiet, a peace that is profound, a happiness that is as steady as the breath. Stillness is the essence of mindfulness, a space where we reconnect with ourselves, where we find clarity, where we experience life in its purest, most beautiful form.

Practices for Cultivating Mindfulness and Present Awareness

Mindfulness is a practice, a journey, a way of being that requires intention, awareness, and love. Below are practices that can help us cultivate mindfulness, that can guide us on the path to present awareness, that can create a life that is rich in joy, in peace, in beauty.

1. Practice Breath Awareness: Focus on your breath, on each inhale, each exhale, each pause. This practice of breath awareness helps to ground you in the present, to calm the mind, to create a sense of peace, of presence.

2. Engage in Sensory Awareness: Take time to notice the details around you, the colours, the sounds, the textures, the tastes, the scents. This practice of sensory awareness helps to heighten your sensitivity to beauty, to find joy in the ordinary, to experience life in its fullness.

3. Let Go of Judgment: Practice accepting each moment as it is, without judgment, without resistance, without the need to control. This practice of non-judgment helps to create a sense of peace, to embrace life with compassion, to experience happiness in acceptance.

4. Create Moments of Stillness: Take time to pause, to be still, to experience the beauty of silence, the peace of stillness, the joy of simply being. This practice of stillness helps to reconnect you with yourself, to find clarity, to find joy in the pause.

5. Practice Gratitude for the Present: Reflect on the beauty of the moment, on the

joy of being alive, on the gift of the present. This practice of gratitude helps to create a sense of appreciation, to inspire a life that is grounded in mindfulness, that is rich in joy, that is full.

The Joy of Mindfulness: A Life That is Fully Alive

Mindfulness is a pathway to happiness, a source of peace, a way of finding joy through presence, through awareness, through love. It is a happiness that is not tied to the past, nor bound by the future, but rooted in the here and now. It is a joy that is as steady as the breath, a contentment that is as gentle as a smile, a peace that is as deep as the soul.

As we continue this journey, may we carry with us the gift of mindfulness, the knowledge that we are capable of experiencing life in its fullness, that we are free to embrace each moment, that we are alive to the beauty of the present.

In the journey of mindfulness, we find a happiness that is deep, a joy that is steady, a peace that is as boundless as the love we hold within.

CHAPTER 20: THE MYSTERY OF AWE – FINDING WONDER IN THE WORLD

Awe is the feeling that fills us when we stand on the edge of the infinite, when we encounter something so beautiful, so vast, so mysterious, that words fall away and we are left only with silence, with wonder, with a profound sense of connection to something greater. Awe is the soul's way of opening itself, of reaching beyond the limits of the mind, of experiencing a happiness that is deep, a joy that is boundless, a peace that is as vast as the universe.

To experience awe is to feel a reverence for the mysteries of life, a respect for the unknown, a humility before the grandeur of existence. It is to be reminded that there is beauty beyond our understanding, that there are wonders beyond our grasp, that there is a vastness within and around us that is as humbling as it is uplifting. In awe, we find not only happiness, but a sense of belonging, a feeling of unity, a love that is as infinite as the stars.

In this chapter, we explore awe as a pathway to happiness, a source of inspiration, a journey into the wonders of the world. For in awe, we discover a happiness that is not about having or knowing, but about being, about experiencing, about allowing ourselves to be touched by the mysteries of life.

The Power of Awe: A Gateway to Inner Expansion

Awe is a gateway to the soul, a doorway that leads us beyond the ordinary, beyond the familiar, beyond ourselves. When we experience awe, we feel a shift within, a softening, an expansion. We are reminded of the vastness of life, the interconnectedness of all things, the beauty that is woven into the very fabric of existence. Awe humbles us, it uplifts us, it opens us to a happiness that is not about fulfilment, but about transcendence.

Imagine standing at the edge of a canyon, looking out over its depths, feeling the immensity of the earth beneath you, the sky above you, the silence around you. In this moment, you are not thinking; you are simply being, simply feeling, simply existing. This is awe—a state of presence, of reverence, of wonder.

In awe, we find a happiness that is quiet, a joy that is pure, a peace that is as deep as the mystery itself. It is a feeling that lifts us beyond ourselves, that connects us to the whole, that reminds us that we are part of something vast, something beautiful, something sacred. Awe is the soul's way of reaching for the infinite, a reminder that happiness is not only a state of being, but a way of seeing, a way of feeling, a way of experiencing life in its fullness.

The Beauty of Nature: A Source of Awe and Wonder

Nature is a masterpiece of awe, a living work of art, a symphony of life that speaks to us in colours, in sounds, in forms that are as mysterious as they are beautiful. To experience nature is to be reminded of the beauty of existence, of the cycles of life, of the harmony that connects all things. In nature, we find a source of awe that is pure, that is unbounded, that is as old as the earth itself.

Imagine the majesty of a mountain, its peaks reaching toward the sky, its slopes carved by time, by wind, by water. Imagine the beauty of a forest, its trees standing tall, its leaves whispering in the breeze, its silence filled with life. Imagine the vastness of the ocean, its waves rolling endlessly, its depths unknown, its beauty timeless. In these moments, we feel a sense of awe, a joy that arises not from understanding, but from experiencing, from being present, from being a part of this incredible world.

Nature reminds us that there is beauty in simplicity, that there is wonder in the smallest details, that there is a joy in simply being. To experience awe in nature is to connect with life itself, to feel a sense of unity, of peace, of happiness that arises from the knowledge that we are part of something vast, something beautiful, something eternal.

The Wonders of Art: A Reflection of the Soul's Depth

Art is another pathway to awe, a mirror of the human spirit, a reflection of our deepest emotions, our highest aspirations, our greatest dreams. Through art, we glimpse the mysteries of the heart, the beauty of the soul, the creativity that flows within each of us. Art is not only a product of the mind; it is an expression of the soul, a language of awe, a way of connecting with something beyond ourselves.

Imagine standing before a painting, feeling the colours, the brushstrokes, the emotion that radiates from the canvas. Imagine listening to a piece of music, feeling each note resonate, each melody unfold, each chord move you, touch you, lift you. Imagine reading a poem, feeling the words sink into your heart, the images bloom in your mind, the meaning resonate in your soul. In these moments, we experience a sense of awe, a joy that is profound, a happiness that is as deep as the art itself.

Art reminds us that beauty is not only in the world, but within us, that wonder is not only in the stars, but in the soul. Through art, we find a pathway to awe, a source of inspiration, a connection to the mysteries of existence. Art is a reminder that we are not only observers of beauty, but creators of it, that we are capable of expressing, of feeling, of experiencing life in ways that are rich, that are meaningful, that are full of wonder.

The Mystery of Life: Embracing the Unknown

Awe is also found in the mysteries of life, in the questions that have no answers, in the experiences that have no explanation, in the moments that defy understanding. To embrace awe is to embrace the unknown, to live with a sense of wonder, to be open to the possibility that there is more to life than we can see, more to existence than we can know, more to the universe than we can comprehend.

To experience awe is to accept that some things cannot be explained, that some mysteries cannot be solved, that some wonders cannot be understood. It is to live with a sense of humility, a respect for the vastness of life, a reverence for the unknown. Awe invites us to let go of the need for answers, to surrender to the mystery, to find joy in the questions, to find peace in the not-knowing.

Imagine looking up at the night sky, seeing the stars scattered across the darkness, feeling the immensity of the universe, the mystery of existence, the beauty of the unknown. In this moment, you feel a sense of awe, a joy that is both humbling and uplifting, a happiness that arises not from knowing, but from wondering, from experiencing, from being present in the face of the infinite.

Practices for Cultivating Awe and Finding Wonder

Awe is a practice, a way of being, a journey that requires openness, presence, and a willingness to be moved. Below are practices that can help us cultivate awe, that can guide us on the path to wonder, that can create a life that is rich in beauty, in joy, in happiness.

1. Spend Time in Nature: Take time to be in nature, to observe its beauty, to connect with its rhythms, to experience its peace. This practice helps to awaken a sense of awe, to create a connection with life, to find joy in the beauty of the earth.

2. Engage with Art: Explore art in its many forms—paintings, music, literature, dance. Allow yourself to be moved, to feel, to experience. This practice of engaging with art helps to awaken the soul, to inspire a sense of wonder, to create a connection with the beauty within and around us.

3. Practice Mindful Presence: Be present in each moment, open to the beauty, the mystery, the wonder that surrounds you. This practice of mindfulness helps to heighten your sensitivity to awe, to find joy in the ordinary, to experience life in its fullness.

4. Embrace the Unknown: Practice living with a sense of curiosity, with a willingness to embrace the unknown, with a respect for the mysteries of life. This practice helps to create a sense of humility, to find joy in the questions, to experience happiness in the not-knowing.

5. Reflect on Moments of Awe: Take time to reflect on the moments when you felt awe, when you experienced wonder, when you were touched by the beauty of life. This reflection helps to reinforce the power of awe, to inspire a life that is rich in wonder, that is filled with joy, that is open to the beauty of existence.

The Joy of Awe: A Happiness That is Boundless

Awe is a pathway to happiness, a source of inspiration, a way of finding joy through wonder, through beauty, through love. It is a happiness that arises not from possession, but from presence, a joy that is not about having, but about experiencing, a peace that is as boundless as the mystery itself.

As we continue this journey, may we carry with us the gift of awe, the knowledge that we are capable of experiencing life in its fullness, that we are free to be moved by the beauty around us, that we are open to the mysteries that surround us.

Through the mystery of awe, we find a happiness that is

deep, a joy that is steady, a peace that is as vast as the universe.

CHAPTER 21: IMPERFECTION AS PERFECTION – EMBRACING FLAWS AS STRENGTHS

To be human is to be beautifully imperfect, a mosaic of strengths and weaknesses, a dance of light and shadow, a symphony of triumphs and trials. Each flaw, each scar, each imperfection is a part of the story we carry, a testament to the life we have lived, a mark of resilience, of growth, of individuality. Perfection is a mirage, a distant illusion; it is in our imperfections that we find our humanity, our strength, our true beauty.

In a world that often values perfection, that chases an ideal, that glorifies flawlessness, embracing our imperfections becomes an act of courage, a path to freedom, a source of joy. To love ourselves as we are is to find peace in authenticity, to recognize the beauty in the cracks, to honour the wisdom in the scars. For in our imperfections, we find not only acceptance, but a happiness that is deep, a contentment that is true, a life that is as real as it is beautiful.

In this chapter, we explore the beauty of imperfection, the strength that arises from embracing our flaws, the joy that comes from honouring our uniqueness. For in embracing our imperfections, we discover a happiness that is unshakable, a peace that is profound, a love that is as boundless as the soul.

The Myth of Perfection: Letting Go of Unrealistic Ideals

Perfection is a myth, a story we tell ourselves, an ideal that we chase but never reach. Society often teaches us that to be worthy, we must be flawless, that to be beautiful, we must be without blemish, that to be successful, we must make no mistakes. But this obsession with perfection is a trap, a source of stress, of insecurity, of unhappiness. Perfection does not make us whole; it makes us hollow, hiding our true selves beneath a mask of ideals that are not our own.

To let go of perfection is to release ourselves from the pressure of unrealistic expectations, to embrace the freedom that comes from being real, from being true, from being human. It is to accept that we are not defined by our flaws, but by our courage to be ourselves, to live with authenticity, to show up in the world as we truly are.

Imagine standing before a cracked piece of pottery, each line a mark of time, a testament to resilience, a reminder that beauty does not lie in flawlessness, but in character, in history, in truth. This is the beauty of imperfection —a beauty that is raw, that is honest, that is real. In embracing imperfection, we find not only peace, but a joy that is steady, a happiness that is rooted, a life that is full.

The Strength in Imperfections: Flaws as Markers of Resilience

Our imperfections are not weaknesses; they are markers of our strength, symbols of the battles we have faced, reminders of the courage it took to endure, to persevere, to grow. Each scar tells a story, each flaw holds a lesson, each imperfection reflects the life we have lived, the struggles we have overcome, the person we have become. To embrace our flaws is to honour our resilience, to recognize the power in our vulnerability, to see the strength in our humanity.

Consider the Japanese art of kintsugi, in which broken pottery is repaired with gold, each crack filled with care, each flaw transformed into something beautiful, something unique, something valuable. In kintsugi, the cracks are not hidden; they are celebrated, they are made visible, they are highlighted as part of the pottery's beauty. In the same way, our flaws are not something to hide, but something to celebrate, something that makes us whole, something that makes us beautiful.

When we embrace our imperfections, we find a strength that is steady, a courage that is quiet, a resilience that is deep. We recognize that we are not defined by our flaws, but by our ability to accept them, to honour them, to see them as a part of our journey. For in our imperfections, we find not only strength, but a happiness that is rooted in self-acceptance, a joy that arises from self-love, a peace that is as enduring as the scars we carry.

The Beauty of Authenticity: Embracing Who We Are

Authenticity is the freedom to be ourselves, to live without pretence, to embrace our true nature, to honour our own journey. To be authentic is to accept ourselves as we are, to recognize that we are enough, to find joy in our own uniqueness, to live with a heart that is open, a spirit that is true, a soul that is whole. In authenticity, we find a happiness that is steady, a peace that is profound, a life that is rich, that is full, that is real.

Imagine a field of wildflowers, each one unique, each one imperfect, each one beautiful in its own way. There is no uniformity, no perfection, no sameness. Yet, together, they create a beauty that is breathtaking, a harmony that is vibrant, a joy that is as boundless as the sky. This is the beauty of authenticity—a beauty that is diverse, that is unique, that is imperfect. In embracing our own authenticity, we find a happiness that is not dependent on approval, but on acceptance, a joy that is not about fitting in, but about standing out, a peace that is as deep as the truth within us.

To embrace our imperfections is to celebrate our individuality, to recognize that our flaws are a part of our beauty, to find joy in our own uniqueness. Authenticity is a reminder that we do not need to be perfect to be beautiful, that we do not need to be flawless to be worthy, that we do not need to change to be loved.

Letting Go of Comparison: Finding Contentment in Our Own Journey

One of the greatest barriers to self-acceptance is comparison, the tendency to measure ourselves against others, to judge our worth based on external standards, to seek validation outside ourselves. Comparison is a thief of joy, a source of insecurity, a trap that keeps us from seeing our own value, our own beauty, our own strengths. To let go of comparison is to find contentment in our own journey, to embrace our own path, to celebrate our own uniqueness.

Imagine walking through a forest, each tree different, each branch unique, each leaf shaped by its own growth, its own journey, its own story. There is no comparison, no judgment, no standard of perfection. Each tree is beautiful in its own way, each tree is perfect in its imperfection, each tree is complete in its own right. In the same way, we are each on our own journey, each growing in our own way, each becoming in our own time.

To let go of comparison is to find peace in our own path, to recognize that we are enough, to honour the beauty of our own story. It is to celebrate our own growth, to embrace our own imperfections, to find happiness in our own journey. For in letting go of comparison, we find a joy that is grounded, a happiness that is steady, a peace that is as constant as the self-acceptance within us.

Practices for Embracing Imperfection and Finding Strength in Flaws

Embracing imperfection is a practice, a journey, a way of living that requires self-compassion, acceptance, and love. Below are practices that can help us embrace our imperfections, that can guide us on the path to self-acceptance, that can create a life that is rich in authenticity, in peace, in happiness.

1. Practice Self-Compassion: Treat yourself with

kindness, with understanding, with love. Embrace your flaws, your mistakes, your imperfections. This practice of self-compassion helps to create a sense of peace, to foster self-acceptance, to cultivate a life that is grounded in self-love.

2. Celebrate Your Unique Qualities: Take time to reflect on the qualities that make you unique, the strengths that arise from your imperfections, the beauty that lies in your individuality. This practice of self-celebration helps to create a sense of pride, to foster a spirit of self-appreciation, to find joy in who you are.

3. Engage in Authentic Self-Expression: Practice expressing yourself authentically, without fear, without pretence, without the need for approval. This practice of authenticity helps to create a sense of freedom, to foster self-confidence, to cultivate a life that is true to your own values, your own heart, your own soul.

4. Release the Need for Perfection: Practice letting go of perfection, of unrealistic standards, of external expectations. Embrace the beauty of your flaws, the strength of your scars, the wisdom of your journey. This practice of release helps to create a sense of liberation, to foster self-acceptance, to find joy in the truth of who you are.

5. Reflect on Your Journey of Growth: Take time to reflect on your journey, on the ways in which you have grown, on the lessons you have learned, on the strength that has arisen from your struggles. This reflection helps to create a sense of gratitude, to honour your journey, to find happiness in the beauty of your own life.

The Joy of Imperfection: A Happiness That is Whole

To embrace imperfection is to find joy in authenticity, to experience happiness through self-acceptance, to discover peace in being real, in being true, in being whole. It is a happiness that is not about flawlessness, but about completeness, a joy that arises not from perfection, but from acceptance, a contentment that is as steady as the heart, as deep as the soul.

As we continue this journey, may we carry with us the courage to embrace our imperfections, the wisdom to honour our flaws, the knowledge that we are beautiful in our own way, that we are strong in our own right, that we are complete as we are.

By the art of embracing imperfection, we find a happiness that is true, a joy that is steady, a peace that is as boundless as the love we hold within.

CHAPTER 22: THE FREEDOM OF FORGIVENESS – HEALING THROUGH RELEASE

Forgiveness is a gift we give ourselves, a release that lifts the weight from our hearts, a path that leads us from pain to peace, from sorrow to serenity, from anger to acceptance. To forgive is not to condone, nor is it to forget; it is to free ourselves from the chains of resentment, to let go of the bitterness that clouds our joy, to create space for love, for healing, for happiness.

Forgiveness is a journey, a process, a practice of softening, of surrender, of opening. It is a way of choosing peace over pain, of finding freedom through release, of experiencing a happiness that is gentle, a joy that is unburdened, a contentment that is deep. For in forgiveness, we discover not only healing, but a sense of wholeness, a freedom that arises not from changing the past, but from accepting it, from releasing it, from letting it be.

In this chapter, we explore forgiveness as a liberating act, a choice that allows us to heal, to grow, to create space for joy. For in forgiveness, we find a happiness that is steady, a peace that is profound, a life that is free from the burdens of anger, of resentment, of regret.

The Burden of Grudges: The Weight of Unresolved Pain

When we hold onto grudges, we carry a weight that grows heavier with time, a burden that limits our joy, that closes our hearts, that dims our light. A grudge is a wound that remains open, a pain that festers, a sorrow that lingers. It keeps us tied to the past, to the hurt, to the anger, preventing us from moving forward, from embracing the fullness of the present, from experiencing the beauty of life.

Holding onto a grudge is like clutching a stone in our hearts, a stone that grows heavier, harder, colder. It drains us of energy, of joy, of peace. We may think that holding onto resentment protects us, but in reality, it imprisons us, it keeps us bound to the very pain we wish to escape, it traps us in a cycle of anger, of sorrow, of bitterness.

To forgive is to release this weight, to set down the stone, to free ourselves from the burden of resentment. It is to choose peace over pain, to let go of the anger, to make space for healing, for joy, for love. For in forgiveness, we find a freedom that is light, a happiness that is gentle, a life that is as open as the heart itself.

The Healing Power of Forgiveness: A Pathway to Wholeness

Forgiveness is not only an act of release; it is a source of healing, a way of mending the wounds within, a path to wholeness, to peace, to happiness. When we forgive, we do not change the past, but we transform our relationship with it, we soften its hold, we find a way to move forward with grace, with compassion, with love.

To forgive is to reclaim our power, to take back the energy we have given to anger, to sorrow, to regret. It is a way of nurturing our own well-being, of choosing love over resentment, of embracing peace over pain. In forgiveness, we find a healing that is gentle, a joy that is deep, a contentment that is as steady as the breath.

Imagine the peace that arises when we let go, the lightness that fills us, the joy that returns to our hearts. This is the healing power of forgiveness—a way of mending our own wounds, of finding solace, of embracing life with an open heart. Forgiveness is not a weakness; it is a strength, a courage, a resilience. It is a reminder that we are capable of choosing peace, of creating joy, of healing ourselves from within.

Letting Go of Resentment: Finding Peace in Release

To let go of resentment is to free ourselves from the grip of anger, from the chains of bitterness, from the prison of the past. Resentment is a fire that burns within, a pain that eats away at our peace, a shadow that clouds our joy. But when we choose to forgive, we put out this fire, we release ourselves from the darkness, we step into the light of freedom, of peace, of happiness.

Letting go of resentment is not about erasing the past; it is about accepting it, about finding peace in what has been, about making space for what is to come. It is a practice of release, a choice to be free, a commitment to live with a heart that is open, a mind that is clear, a spirit that is light.

Imagine a garden that has been neglected, its soil filled with stones, its flowers choked by weeds. Resentment is like these stones, these weeds, blocking the growth of joy, of peace, of love. But when we forgive, we clear the soil, we remove the stones, we make room for beauty, for growth, for life. Forgiveness is a way of tending to our own hearts, of creating a space where happiness can bloom, where peace can grow, where love can flourish.

The Joy of Release: Creating Space for Happiness

Forgiveness is an act of liberation, a way of creating space within, a path to happiness, to joy, to peace. When we forgive, we do not lose; we gain. We gain a lightness of spirit, a freedom of heart, a joy that arises from the release of pain, from the surrender of sorrow, from the acceptance of what is.

Imagine the feeling of setting down a heavy bag after a long journey, the relief, the freedom, the sense of release. This is the joy of forgiveness—a lightness, a peace, a happiness that comes from letting go, from releasing the burdens we carry, from freeing ourselves to live, to love, to be.

Forgiveness is a way of opening ourselves to joy, of creating a space within for happiness, of making room for love, for peace, for beauty. It is a reminder that we are not defined by our pain, but by our ability to release it, that we are not bound by our past, but free to embrace the present, that we are not held back by anger, but lifted by love.

Practices for Cultivating Forgiveness and Finding Freedom

Forgiveness is a practice, a journey, a way of being that requires compassion, presence, and love. Below are practices that can help us embrace forgiveness, that can guide us on the path to healing, that can create a life that is rich in peace, in joy, in freedom.

1. Practice Self-Compassion: Begin by forgiving yourself, by treating yourself with kindness, by accepting your own imperfections. This practice of self-compassion helps to create a foundation of love, to foster self-acceptance, to cultivate a life that is grounded in self-forgiveness.

2. Release the Need for Control: Forgiveness is a surrender, a release, a letting go. Practice releasing the need to control the past, to change what has been, to hold onto pain. This practice of release helps to create a sense of freedom, to foster inner peace, to find joy in the present.

3. Engage in Mindful Reflection: Take time to reflect on the burdens you carry, the grudges you hold, the pain that lingers. This practice of mindful reflection helps to bring awareness to the need for forgiveness, to inspire a spirit of release, to create a life that is free from the past.

4. Visualize the Joy of Forgiveness: Imagine the lightness, the peace, the happiness that comes from forgiveness. Visualize yourself setting down the weight, freeing yourself from resentment, embracing a life that is light,

that is open, that is full. This visualization helps to create a sense of motivation, to inspire a commitment to forgiveness, to foster a life that is rich in joy.

5. Practice Gratitude for the Present: Focus on the beauty of the present, on the gifts of the now, on the joy of being alive. This practice of gratitude helps to shift your focus from the past to the present, to create a sense of peace, to inspire a life that is grounded in forgiveness, that is open to happiness.

The Freedom of Forgiveness: A Life That is Full

Forgiveness is a pathway to happiness, a source of healing, a way of finding peace through release, through surrender, through love. It is a happiness that is not bound by the past, but rooted in the present, a joy that arises not from holding on, but from letting go, a peace that is as gentle as a sigh, as profound as the heart.

As we continue this journey, may we carry with us the gift of forgiveness, the knowledge that we are capable of releasing the past, of embracing the present, of creating a life that is free, that is light, that is full.

In the freedom of forgiveness, we find a happiness that is deep, a joy that is steady, a peace that is as boundless as the love we hold within.

CHAPTER 23: RITUALS FOR HAPPINESS – DAILY PRACTICES TO CULTIVATE JOY

Happiness is not only found in grand achievements or rare moments; it resides in the quiet rituals, the small acts, the daily practices that we weave into our lives with intention, with love, with presence. Rituals are the anchors of happiness, the steady rhythms that ground us, the gentle reminders to return to ourselves, to connect with the world, to nourish our souls. Through rituals, we cultivate joy in the everyday, we create moments of peace, we embrace life with gratitude, with mindfulness, with delight.

To establish rituals for happiness is to invite joy into the ordinary, to find beauty in the simple, to experience each day as an opportunity to nurture our well-being. Rituals do not require elaborate preparation or grand gestures; they are often the smallest acts, done with intention, with care, with love. They are the morning stretches that awaken the body, the evening gratitude that calms the heart, the deep breaths that ground the spirit.

In this chapter, we explore the power of daily rituals, the ways in which simple practices can cultivate joy, the beauty that arises when we live with intention, with mindfulness, with love. For in these rituals, we find a happiness that is steady, a joy that is enduring, a life that is rich in moments of peace, of beauty, of contentment.

The Power of Rituals: Anchoring Happiness in the Everyday

Rituals are more than habits; they are acts of reverence, of presence, of care. While habits may be mindless, rituals are mindful, infused to bring meaning, to foster joy, to ground us in the here and now. Through rituals, we create a rhythm that steadies us, that soothes us, that brings joy into the ordinary, that transforms the mundane into the sacred.

Imagine the comfort of lighting a candle in the evening, the warmth of its glow, the calm of its light, the sense of peace that fills the room. This small act, this simple ritual, creates a moment of beauty, a pause in the day, a reminder to slow down, to breathe, to be. This is the power of rituals—a way of creating happiness through presence, of finding joy in intention, of nurturing the soul through the beauty of the everyday.

To establish rituals is to honour our own well-being, to give ourselves the gift of peace, to create a life that is filled with moments of happiness, with practices of joy, with acts of love. Rituals are the seeds of happiness, planted with intention, watered with presence, grown with care.

Morning Rituals: Beginning the Day with Joy and Intention

The morning is a time of new beginnings, a fresh start, a chance to greet the day with gratitude, with presence, with joy. Morning rituals are a way of setting the tone, of creating a foundation of happiness, of beginning the day with intention. Through these rituals, we awaken not only the body, but the mind, the heart, the spirit.

Imagine waking up each day with a moment of stillness, a deep breath, a gentle stretch. Imagine beginning the day with gratitude, a quiet acknowledgment of the beauty of being alive, the gift of another day, the joy of new possibilities. This is the essence of morning rituals— a practice of presence, a way of grounding ourselves, a moment of peace that carries us into the day.

Morning rituals do not need to be elaborate; they can be as simple as a few minutes of meditation, a warm cup of tea, a mindful breath. The beauty of morning rituals is in their simplicity, their ease, their ability to bring joy into the beginning of each day, to create a life that is rich in intention, in peace, in happiness.

Midday Rituals: Moments of Pause and Rejuvenation

In the midst of a busy day, rituals serve as pauses, as breaths, as moments of return. Midday rituals are a way of stepping back, of reconnecting with ourselves, of finding calm amidst the chaos. They are the moments when we pause to nourish our bodies, to calm our minds, to reconnect with the present.

Imagine taking a few moments during the day to close your eyes, to take a deep breath, to feel the tension melt away, to find peace in the pause. Or imagine enjoying a mindful lunch, savouring each bite, feeling gratitude for the nourishment, the energy, the joy of food. These are the midday rituals that ground us, that rejuvenate us, that bring happiness into the heart of the day.

Midday rituals are reminders to slow down, to breathe, to take care of ourselves. They are moments of self-care, acts of love, practices of presence. Through these rituals, we find a happiness that is steady, a peace that is calming, a life that is filled with moments of joy, of rejuvenation, of contentment.

Evening Rituals: Embracing Calm and Reflecting with Gratitude

The evening is a time of rest, of reflection, of release. Evening rituals are a way of winding down, of letting go of the day, of embracing peace, of preparing for sleep with a heart that is calm, a mind that is clear, a spirit that is at ease. Through evening rituals, we find closure, we create a sense of peace, we drift into rest with gratitude, with contentment, with love.

Imagine ending each day with a few moments of gratitude, a quiet reflection on the joys, the lessons, the moments of beauty. Or imagine reading a few pages of a favourite book, allowing the words to soothe, to inspire, to calm. Evening rituals are not about doing more; they are about doing less, about creating space, about allowing ourselves to rest, to reflect, to be.

Evening rituals are a gentle reminder that happiness is

found in the quiet moments, in the acts of letting go, in the practice of gratitude. They are a way of embracing the peace of the night, of honouring the end of the day, of creating a life that is filled with moments of calm, of reflection, of joy.

Mindfulness in Rituals: Bringing Presence into Each Practice

Mindfulness is the heart of rituals, the essence of happiness, the way in which we bring presence, intention, and love into each moment. To be mindful is to be fully alive, to be fully engaged, to be fully present. Mindfulness transforms rituals from routine to reverence, from habit to healing, from action to art.

Imagine brushing your teeth with mindfulness, feeling the sensation of the water, the taste of the toothpaste, the movement of your hand. Or imagine washing your hands with presence, feeling the warmth of the water, the softness of the soap, the refreshment of the ritual. These small acts, these everyday moments, become sources of joy, of peace, of happiness.

Through mindfulness, we create a life that is rich in beauty, in presence, in joy. We find happiness not in the grand, but in the simple, not in the extraordinary, but in the ordinary, not in the future, but in the now. Mindfulness is a way of making each ritual a source of happiness, a practice of joy, a moment of love.

Practices for Creating Rituals of Happiness and Joy

Creating rituals is a practice, a journey, a way of living that requires intention, presence, and love. Below are practices that can help us create rituals, that can guide us on the path to happiness, that can nurture a life that is rich in peace, in joy, in fulfilment.

1. Begin the Day with Gratitude: Take a few moments each morning to reflect on what you are grateful for, to honour the beauty of a new day, to embrace the joy of being alive. This ritual of gratitude helps to create a foundation of happiness, to set a tone of joy, to foster a life that is grounded in appreciation.

2. Incorporate Mindful Breathing: Practice mindful breathing throughout the day, taking a few deep breaths, focusing on the inhale, the exhale, the pause. This ritual of mindful breathing helps to create a sense of calm, to ground you in the present, to foster a life that is rich in peace.

3. Engage in Mindful Eating: Take time to savour each meal, to enjoy each bite, to experience the flavours, the textures, the nourishment. This ritual of mindful eating helps to create a sense of presence, to honour the body, to foster a life that is filled with gratitude, with joy, with appreciation.

4. End the Day with Reflection: Take a few moments each evening to reflect on the day, to honour the joys, the lessons, the moments of beauty. This ritual of reflection helps to create a sense of closure, to foster gratitude, to embrace peace.

5. Create Moments of Stillness: Take time each day to be still, to be quiet, to simply be. This ritual of stillness helps to create a sense of calm, to foster mindfulness, to cultivate a life that is rich in peace, in joy, in presence.

The Joy of Rituals: A Life That is Full

Rituals are the heart of happiness, the essence of peace, the source of joy. Through rituals, we create a life that is grounded in presence, a happiness that is rooted in intention, a joy that is as gentle as the breath, as steady as the heart, as profound as the soul.

As we continue this journey, may we carry with us the power of rituals, the knowledge that we are capable of creating moments of happiness, that we are free to cultivate joy, that we are open to the beauty of the everyday.

Through this, we find a life that is rich, a joy that is steady, a peace that is as boundless as the love we hold within.

CHAPTER 24: SERENITY OF ACCEPTANCE – FINDING PEACE WITH LIFE'S TRANSIENCE

Acceptance is the quiet wisdom of the heart, a gentle surrender to the flow of life, a path that leads us from resistance to peace, from worry to calm, from fear to freedom. To accept is not to give up, nor is it to resign; it is to embrace life as it is, to honour the journey, to recognize the beauty in impermanence, to find serenity in the transience of all things. Through acceptance, we discover a happiness that is steady, a peace that is deep, a love that is as boundless as the sky.

Life is a river that flows, a season that changes, a moment that comes and goes. To live with acceptance is to flow with this river, to dance in this season, to embrace each moment without clinging, without grasping, without fear. Acceptance is a way of finding freedom in transience, of seeing beauty in change, of experiencing life with a heart that is open, a mind that is clear, a soul that is at ease.

In this chapter, we explore acceptance as a pathway to peace, a source of serenity, a way of embracing life's fleeting nature without fear, without regret, without sorrow. For in acceptance, we find a happiness that is not dependent on permanence, a joy that is not bound by control, a contentment that is as steady as the earth, as vast as the sky, as timeless as the soul.

The Impermanence of Life: Embracing the Beauty of Change

Life is a dance of change, a rhythm of beginnings and endings, a cycle of birth, growth, decay, and rebirth. Everything is in motion, everything is evolving, everything is becoming. To resist this change is to resist life itself, to cling to what was, to fear what will be, to miss the beauty of what is. Acceptance is the art of letting go, the wisdom of seeing the beauty in impermanence, the serenity of embracing life as a journey, a flow, a mystery.

Imagine the petals of a flower, blooming in the morning sun, wilting as the day fades, falling as the night descends. There is a beauty in this cycle, a grace in this change, a peace in this impermanence. Life, too, is like this flower, a series of moments that bloom and fade, each one unique, each one precious, each one complete in its own way.

To embrace the impermanence of life is to see each

moment as a gift, each change as an opportunity, each ending as a doorway to something new. It is to live with a heart that is open to the flow, a spirit that is free from fear, a mind that is grounded in peace. For in acceptance, we find a happiness that is not dependent on permanence, but on presence, a joy that is not about holding on, but about letting go, a serenity that is as timeless as the moment itself.

The Freedom of Letting Go: Releasing Control to Find Peace

To let go is to release the need to control, to surrender the illusion of permanence, to trust in the journey, to embrace the flow of life. When we cling to the past, we bind ourselves to what was; when we fear the future, we close ourselves to what will be. But when we let go, we open ourselves to the beauty of what is, we find freedom in acceptance, we experience peace in surrender.

Letting go is not a loss; it is a liberation, a relief, a release. It is the act of setting down the weights we carry, of freeing ourselves from the burdens of worry, of finding joy in the lightness of being. Imagine the feeling of putting down a heavy bag after a long journey, the relief, the ease, the peace that arises. This is the freedom of letting go—a happiness that is light, a joy that is free, a serenity that arises from release, from surrender, from trust.

To let go is to recognize that we cannot control life's flow, that we cannot cling to what is fleeting, that we cannot hold onto what must pass. It is to embrace the truth of impermanence, to live with a heart that is unburdened, a mind that is clear, a soul that is at peace. For in letting go, we find a happiness that is steady, a peace that is profound, a life that is full of freedom, of ease, of joy.

Living with Presence: Finding Joy in the Here and Now

Presence is the essence of acceptance, the practice of being fully here, fully alive, fully aware. To live with presence is to embrace each moment as it comes, to experience life in its fullness, to find joy in the here and now. It is to see the beauty in the fleeting, the richness in the ordinary, the wonder in the moment.

Imagine watching a sunset, the colours changing, the light fading, the night descending. In this moment, there is no past, there is no future, there is only now, only this, only the beauty of the present. To live with presence is to live with a heart that is open to this beauty, a mind that is attentive to this moment, a spirit that is alive to the joy of being.

Presence is a practice, a way of grounding ourselves in the now, a way of finding happiness that is rooted in the moment, a way of experiencing peace that is not dependent on the future, but on the present. Through presence, we embrace life as it is, we find joy in each breath, we experience the serenity of acceptance.

Acceptance as a Source of Inner Peace: The Serenity of Surrender

Acceptance is a source of peace, a path to serenity, a way of finding calm amidst the changes, the losses, the uncertainties of life. It is the practice of surrender, the wisdom of embracing life's flow, the courage to live with an open heart, a clear mind, a soul that is at ease.

To accept is to make peace with what is, to find contentment in the reality of the moment, to experience happiness that is rooted in presence, in trust, in surrender. Acceptance does not mean giving up; it means choosing peace, it means living with grace, it means finding joy in the simplicity of being.

Imagine a tree that stands in a field, its roots deep, its branches reaching toward the sky, its leaves dancing in the wind. The tree does not resist the wind; it bends, it sways, it moves with the flow. This is the serenity of acceptance—a way of being that is grounded, that is open, that is free. Through acceptance, we find a happiness that is steady, a peace that is constant, a life that is rich in moments of calm, of clarity, of joy.

Practices for Cultivating Acceptance and Embracing Life's Transience

Acceptance is a practice, a journey, a way of living that requires presence, awareness, and love. Below are practices that can help us cultivate acceptance, that can guide us on the path to peace, that can create a life that is rich in serenity, in joy, in freedom.

1. Practice Mindful Breathing: Focus on each breath, on the inhale, the exhale, the pause. This practice of mindful breathing helps to ground you in the present, to create a sense of calm, to foster a life that is rooted in acceptance, in presence, in peace.

2. Embrace Impermanence in Nature: Spend time in nature, observing the cycles of growth, of change, of renewal. This practice helps to remind us of life's transience, to inspire a spirit of acceptance, to create a

connection with the flow of life.

3. Release the Need for Control: Practice letting go of the need to control the future, to cling to the past, to resist what is. This practice of release helps to create a sense of freedom, to foster inner peace, to embrace life as it is.

4. Cultivate Gratitude for the Present: Take time to appreciate the beauty of the moment, to honour the joy of the now, to find happiness in the simplicity of being. This practice of gratitude helps to ground you in the present, to create a life that is rich in acceptance, in joy, in peace.

5. Reflect on Life's Transience: Take time to reflect on the impermanence of life, on the beauty of change, on the wisdom of acceptance. This reflection helps to create a sense of peace, to inspire a spirit of acceptance, to foster a life that is rooted in presence, in serenity, in joy.

The Peace of Acceptance: A Life That is Free

Acceptance is a pathway to happiness, a source of serenity, a way of finding peace through presence, through surrender, through love. It is a happiness that is not bound by permanence, but by presence, a joy that arises not from control, but from freedom, a contentment that is as steady as the heart, as deep as the soul, as vast as the sky.

As we continue this journey, may we carry with us the gift of acceptance, the knowledge that we are capable of finding peace in the present, that we are free to embrace life as it is, that we are open to the beauty of change, of transience, of impermanence.

For in the serenity of acceptance, we find a happiness that

is deep, a joy that is steady, a peace that is as boundless as the love we hold within.

CHAPTER 25: CREATIVITY AS CATHARSIS – HEALING THROUGH SELF-EXPRESSION

Creativity is the language of the soul, a form of self-expression that transcends words, a way of giving shape to the unspoken, a channel through which we release our emotions, our dreams, our deepest truths. To create is to open ourselves, to pour our essence into the world, to find healing in the act of making, of expressing, of becoming. Through creativity, we process emotions, we transform pain into beauty, we discover joy in the act of creation.

Artistic expression is not only about producing something beautiful; it is about finding release, experiencing catharsis, embracing the freedom to express ourselves without fear, without judgment, without constraint. Creativity allows us to explore the hidden landscapes of our hearts, to give voice to the unexpressed, to find peace in the act of creation. It is a journey of self-discovery, a process of healing, a path to joy.

In this chapter, we explore the healing power of creativity, the ways in which artistic self-expression serves as a catharsis, a liberation, a joy. For in creativity, we find a happiness that is profound, a peace that is liberating, a life that is rich in colour, in beauty, in meaning.

The Power of Creative Expression: A Pathway to Emotional Release

To create is to release, to let go, to pour our emotions into something tangible, something real, something that carries a part of us. Creative expression is a way of processing our feelings, of transforming our pain, our joy, our wonder into art, into words, into movement. It is a way of turning our inner world into something visible, something we can see, something we can understand.

Imagine the act of painting, each brushstroke a release, each colour an emotion, each line a story. Or imagine writing, each word a truth, each sentence a piece of the self, each paragraph a journey. Creativity is a way of bringing our emotions to the surface, of giving them form, of finding peace in the act of expressing what is within.

Through creative expression, we find a catharsis, a way of freeing ourselves from the weight of unspoken emotions, a release that brings peace, a healing that is profound. To create is to find a happiness that arises not from perfection, but from expression, a joy that comes not from the product, but from the process, a contentment that is as deep as the act itself.

The Healing Art of Transformation: Turning Pain into Beauty

Creativity is a way of transforming pain into beauty, of turning sorrow into art, of making something beautiful from what hurts, what wounds, what challenges us. When we create, we take our experiences, our struggles, our losses, and we transform them into something that heals, that soothes, that uplifts. Creativity is a form of alchemy, a process of turning the lead of pain into the gold of art, a way of finding meaning in the midst of suffering.

Imagine a poet who writes about heartbreak, each line a release, each word a piece of healing, each poem a way of transforming sorrow into something beautiful. Or imagine a dancer who expresses grief through movement, each step a journey, each gesture a release, each dance a path to peace. This is the power of creativity —a way of giving shape to what cannot be spoken, a way of finding beauty in the midst of pain, a way of healing through self-expression.

To transform pain into beauty is to find a happiness that is resilient, a joy that arises from resilience, a peace that is rooted in the strength to create, to express, to transform. For in creativity, we find a healing that is deep, a peace that is profound, a happiness that arises from the act of making, of becoming, of releasing.

The Joy of Creation: Finding Freedom in the Process

Creation is a source of joy, a freedom, a liberation. To create is to be free from expectation, from judgment, from the need to be perfect. It is a journey into ourselves, a way of discovering who we are, a way of expressing our true selves. Creativity allows us to be imperfect, to be messy, to be real. It is not about the product; it is about the process, the joy of making, the freedom of expressing, the happiness of being.

Imagine a child painting with abandon, colours splashing, lines flowing, joy radiating. There is no fear, no judgment, no concern for the end result. This is the joy of creation—a happiness that is pure, a freedom that is boundless, a peace that arises from the act of expressing without restraint, without fear, without limitation.

To create is to return to this state of joy, to embrace the freedom of self-expression, to find peace in the process, to discover a happiness that is as light as a brushstroke, as free as a melody, as boundless as the imagination. For in creativity, we find a life that is full of joy, of freedom, of expression.

Creativity as Self-Discovery: Uncovering the Depths of the Soul

Creativity is a journey of self-discovery, a way of exploring our inner world, of uncovering the layers of the self, of finding truth in the act of expression. When we create, we are not only making something external; we are also discovering something internal. We are uncovering the truths that lie within, the emotions that linger, the dreams that call us. Creativity is a way of connecting with our own soul, a process of understanding who we are, a path to self-awareness.

Imagine writing in a journal, each word a revelation, each sentence a piece of the self, each page a journey inward. Or imagine sculpting, each curve a reflection of the soul, each line a truth, each shape a part of the inner world. Creativity is a way of uncovering the self, of bringing to light the parts of us that are hidden, of finding peace in the act of self-discovery.

Through creativity, we find a happiness that is deep, a joy that is true, a life that is rich in meaning, in connection, in awareness. To create is to know oneself, to express oneself, to love oneself. For in creativity, we find a path to self-discovery, a journey into the heart, a connection with the soul.

Practices for Cultivating Creativity and Finding Healing in Expression

Creativity is a practice, a journey, a way of living that requires openness, presence, and love. Below are practices that can help us embrace creativity, that can guide us on the path to healing, that can create a life that is rich in expression, in joy, in freedom.

1. Engage in Free Writing: Take time each day to write freely, without judgment, without structure, without restraint. This practice of free writing helps to create a sense of release, to foster self-expression, to cultivate a life that is grounded in creativity, in freedom, in joy.

2. Express Emotions through Art: Use art as a way of expressing emotions, of releasing pain, of finding healing. This practice of artistic expression helps to create a sense of catharsis, to foster emotional

processing, to embrace creativity as a path to peace.

3. Dance as a Form of Release: Use movement as a way of releasing emotions, of finding freedom, of connecting with the body. This practice of dance helps to create a sense of joy, to foster a connection with the self, to find healing through movement, through expression, through creation.

4. Practice Mindful Drawing or Painting: Use drawing or painting as a form of mindfulness, a way of grounding yourself in the present, of connecting with the moment, of finding peace in the act of creating. This practice helps to create a sense of calm, to foster presence, to embrace creativity as a source of happiness, of healing, of serenity.

5. Explore Music or Sound as Self-Expression: Use music, whether listening or creating, as a way of expressing emotions, of finding joy, of experiencing the catharsis of sound. This practice of musical expression helps to create a sense of connection, to foster emotional release, to find peace in the rhythm, the melody, the harmony of creativity.

The Healing Power of Creativity: A Life That is Full

Creativity is a path to happiness, a source of healing, a way of finding joy through self-expression, through release, through creation. It is a happiness that arises not from perfection, but from presence, a joy that is not about the product, but about the process, a contentment that is as deep as the soul, as free as the spirit, as boundless as the heart.

As we continue this journey, may we carry with us the gift of creativity, the knowledge that we are capable of expressing ourselves, that we are free to create, that we are open to the beauty of self-expression.

In the catharsis of creativity, we find a happiness that is deep, a joy that is true, a peace that is as boundless as the love we hold within.

CHAPTER 26: WISDOM FROM ANCIENT CULTURES – LESSONS IN TIMELESS HAPPINESS

In the vast expanse of human history, countless cultures have pondered the nature of happiness, seeking paths to peace, contentment, and fulfilment. Across time and geography, ancient wisdom has flowed through the traditions of India, Greece, China, Africa, and beyond, each culture a river of insight, each philosophy a pathway to joy. The wisdom of these ancient cultures reminds us that happiness is not a modern invention; it is an eternal quest, a timeless journey, a pursuit that echoes across generations, across landscapes, across hearts.

To explore these teachings is to connect with a deep well of knowledge, a timeless wisdom that speaks to our souls, that reminds us of our shared humanity, that guides us toward a life of simplicity, of peace, of meaning. These philosophies invite us to live with intention, to embrace the beauty of balance, to seek harmony with ourselves, with others, with the world. They teach us that happiness is not something we chase, but something we cultivate, something we become, something we find within.

In this chapter, we delve into the wisdom of ancient cultures, drawing lessons from timeless philosophies that continue to illuminate the path to happiness. For in the echoes of these traditions, we find a happiness that is deep, a peace that is profound, a joy that is as steady as the mountains, as vast as the sky, as enduring as the soul.

The Indian Philosophy of Contentment: Finding Joy Within

The ancient wisdom of India teaches that true happiness arises from within, that contentment is the key to a life of peace, that joy is found not in the external, but in the internal. The yogic and Vedic philosophies of India emphasize self-awareness, meditation, and inner peace as pathways to happiness, reminding us that when we turn inward, we discover a richness that transcends the material, a joy that is as infinite as the self.

In the Bhagavad Gita, an ancient Indian scripture, there is a teaching that speaks to this wisdom: "The mind that is steady in itself is like a flame undisturbed by the wind." This is the essence of Indian philosophy—a happiness that is steady, a peace that is unwavering, a life that is grounded in inner stillness.

To embrace this wisdom is to seek contentment in simplicity, to find joy in being rather than in possessing, to cultivate a life that is rich in presence, in peace, in purpose. For in the teachings of India, we find a happiness that is steady, a joy that is true, a peace that is as vast as the inner world.

The Greek Philosophy of Eudaimonia: Living with Purpose and Virtue

In ancient Greece, philosophers like Aristotle spoke of eudaimonia, often translated as "flourishing" or "the good life." This concept of happiness is not about pleasure or material success; it is about living in alignment with one's virtues, about finding purpose, about cultivating a life that is meaningful. Eudaimonia is a happiness that arises from living well, from acting with integrity, from becoming the best version of oneself.

Aristotle believed that true happiness was found through a life of purpose, through actions that align with our highest values, through a journey of growth, of self-discovery, of excellence. He taught that happiness is not a fleeting emotion, but a state of being that arises from living a life of virtue, a life that is guided by wisdom, by kindness, by courage.

To embrace the Greek philosophy of eudaimonia is to live with intention, to seek purpose, to cultivate virtues that nourish the soul. It is to find happiness in the journey of becoming, to experience joy in the pursuit of excellence, to find peace in living a life that is rich in meaning, in depth, in integrity. For in the teachings of Greece, we find a happiness that is profound, a joy that is fulfilling, a life that is as steady as the pursuit of virtue itself.

The Chinese Philosophy of Harmony: Embracing Balance and Flow

The ancient philosophy of Taoism in China teaches the wisdom of wu wei, or "effortless action," a way of being that flows with the natural rhythms of life, that embraces balance, that finds peace in harmony. To live in accordance with Taoist wisdom is to move with life rather than against it, to let go of resistance, to embrace the flow. It is a happiness that is not about striving, but about being, not about control, but about acceptance.

Laozi, the ancient sage and author of the Tao Te Ching, speaks of happiness as a way of aligning with the Tao, the natural way of the universe, a path that is gentle, that is flexible, that is open. In his words, "When I let go of what I am, I become what I might be." This is the essence of Taoism—a happiness that is found in surrender, a peace that arises from harmony, a life that flows with grace.

To embrace this wisdom is to live with balance, to find joy in simplicity, to experience peace in acceptance. It is to cultivate a life that is aligned with nature, that honours the rhythms of existence, that finds happiness in harmony, in ease, in flow. For in the teachings of China, we find a happiness that is gentle, a joy that is natural, a peace that is as fluid as the river, as steady as the earth, as vast as the sky.

The African Philosophy of Ubuntu: Finding Happiness in Community

The African philosophy of Ubuntu teaches that happiness

is not an individual pursuit, but a communal one, that we find joy not only in ourselves but in others, that we are interconnected, interdependent, intertwined. Ubuntu is often expressed as "I am because we are", a reminder that our happiness is linked to the happiness of others, that our well-being is connected to the well-being of the community, that our lives are enriched by connection, by compassion, by shared humanity.

In the spirit of Ubuntu, we are encouraged to live with empathy, to extend kindness, to foster a sense of belonging. Happiness, according to this wisdom, is found not in isolation, but in unity, not in self-interest, but in selflessness, not in taking, but in giving. Ubuntu teaches us that to be truly happy, we must honour our connections, embrace our shared humanity, celebrate the joy of community.

To embrace Ubuntu is to find happiness in compassion, to experience joy in connection, to cultivate a life that is rich in love, in kindness, in unity. For in the teachings of Africa, we find a happiness that is shared, a joy that is collective, a peace that is as wide as the community, as deep as compassion, as boundless as love.

The Native American Philosophy of Respect for Nature: Honouring the Earth and Its Gifts

Many Native American cultures hold a deep reverence for nature, a respect for the earth, an understanding that happiness is found in harmony with the natural world. The teachings of Native American wisdom remind us that we are not separate from nature; we are a part of it, connected to the animals, the plants, the rivers, the stars. To live with respect for nature is to find happiness in simplicity, to honour the earth's gifts, to live with gratitude, with humility, with awareness.

In Native American traditions, the earth is seen as a mother, a provider, a source of life. Happiness is found not in possessing, but in giving back, not in consuming, but in conserving, not in isolation, but in connection. To live with respect for nature is to embrace a life of balance, of reverence, of gratitude.

To embrace this wisdom is to find happiness in simplicity, to cultivate a life that is rich in respect, in stewardship, in love for the earth. For in the teachings of Native America, we find a happiness that is grounded, a joy that is harmonious, a peace that is as steady as the mountains, as gentle as the breeze, as enduring as the earth itself.

Practices for Integrating Ancient Wisdom into Modern Life

The wisdom of ancient cultures is timeless, a source of happiness, a path to peace, a guide to a life that is rich in meaning, in joy, in fulfilment. Below are practices that can help us integrate this wisdom into our daily lives, that can create a life that is grounded in ancient principles, that is filled with timeless happiness.

1. Practice Self-Reflection and Meditation: Embrace the Indian tradition of introspection and meditation to cultivate inner peace, to find contentment within, to ground yourself in self-awareness. This practice helps to create a life that is rich in inner calm, in presence, in joy.

2. Live with Purpose and Virtue: Follow the Greek philosophy of eudaimonia by living with purpose, by

aligning your actions with your values, by cultivating virtues that nourish the soul. This practice helps to create a life that is meaningful, that is fulfilling, that is rich in integrity, in purpose, in joy.

3. Embrace Balance and Flow: Follow the Taoist principle of wu wei by embracing balance, by letting go of control, by moving with the flow of life. This practice helps to create a life that is grounded in harmony, in peace, in joy.

4. Foster Connections and Compassion: Practice Ubuntu by fostering connections, by living with empathy, by celebrating community. This practice helps to create a life that is rich in love, in compassion, in shared happiness.

5. Honour Nature and Live with Gratitude: Follow the Native American wisdom of respecting nature by living with gratitude, by honouring the earth, by embracing simplicity. This practice helps to create a life that is grounded, that is harmonious, that is rich in respect, in stewardship, in joy.

The Timeless Happiness of Ancient Wisdom: A Life That is Full

The wisdom of ancient cultures is a gift, a reminder that happiness is not a fleeting pleasure, but a way of being, a journey of the heart, a path to a life that is full. Through these teachings, we find a happiness that is deep, a peace that is profound, a joy that is as timeless as the soul.

As we continue this journey, may we carry with us the wisdom of those who came before, the knowledge that happiness is found in simplicity, in purpose, in connection, in harmony, in gratitude. For in the timeless wisdom of ancient cultures, we find a happiness that is eternal, a joy that is true, a peace that is as boundless as the love we hold within.

CHAPTER 27:
THE ENIGMA
OF THE SELF –
UNDERSTANDING
IDENTITY AND
HAPPINESS

Who am I? This question has echoed through centuries, traversing the hearts and minds of poets, philosophers, and seekers of truth. The self is an enigma, a mysterious mosaic of memories, beliefs, desires, and dreams, a layered essence that is both familiar and elusive. To know oneself is a journey as profound as it is personal, a pilgrimage into the depths of one's own being, a path that leads to understanding, acceptance, and, ultimately, happiness.

To seek the self is not only to understand one's identity but to embrace it, to honour the complexities, to recognize the beauty in the flaws, the strength in the vulnerabilities, the wholeness in the fragments. The journey inward is a discovery of authenticity, a process of peeling away the masks, of letting go of the illusions, of finding the courage to live as we truly are. For happiness, at its core, is rooted in self-acceptance, in the freedom to be one's authentic self, in the joy of embracing one's unique essence.

In this chapter, we explore the enigma of the self, the ways in which self-understanding leads to happiness, the journey of identity that calls us to go within, to reflect, to discover. For in knowing ourselves, we find a happiness that is deep, a peace that is unwavering, a life that is rich in authenticity, in clarity, in joy.

The Layers of Identity: Uncovering the Many Selves Within

Identity is not a single, static concept; it is a tapestry woven from countless threads—our experiences, our relationships, our dreams, our fears, our values. Each layer of the self tells a story, each part of the identity holds a truth, each fragment of the soul reveals a piece of who we are. To understand oneself is to explore these layers, to honour the complexity, to recognize that we are not one thing, but many, not simple, but intricate, not fixed, but evolving.

Imagine peeling an onion, each layer revealing another, each part leading deeper, each peel uncovering a truth. Identity is like this—each layer a part of the self, each one meaningful, each one necessary. The outer layers may be the roles we play, the labels we wear, the personas we show to the world. But as we journey inward, we move beyond these layers, we uncover the essence, we reach the core, the authentic self that lies at the heart of our being.

To explore these layers is to embrace the complexity of identity, to honour each part of ourselves, to see beauty in the wholeness. It is to accept that we are many things at once—strength and vulnerability, hope and fear, light and shadow. For in understanding the layers of the self, we find a happiness that is grounded in self-acceptance, a peace that arises from wholeness, a life that is rich in authenticity.

The Journey Inward: Finding Truth in Self-Reflection

The journey of self-understanding is a journey inward, a path that requires courage, introspection, and honesty. To know oneself is to reflect, to question, to listen to the quiet voice within, to uncover the truths that lie hidden beneath the surface. Self-reflection is a mirror through which we see our own soul, a practice that brings clarity, that fosters understanding, that illuminates the mysteries of the self.

Imagine sitting by a still lake, the water reflecting the sky, the trees, the soul. In this stillness, we see ourselves as we are, without distortion, without pretence, without fear. Self-reflection is like this lake, a mirror that reveals the truth, a space that invites honesty, a practice that brings peace.

Through self-reflection, we uncover our values, our dreams, our fears, our desires. We come to understand what drives us, what fulfils us, what brings us joy. We learn to honour our strengths, to accept our weaknesses, to embrace the truth of who we are. For in self-reflection, we find a happiness that arises from understanding, a joy that is rooted in authenticity, a peace that comes from knowing and accepting oneself.

Embracing Authenticity: The Freedom to Be Oneself

To be authentic is to live in alignment with one's true self, to embrace one's unique essence, to express oneself without fear, without pretence, without the need for approval. Authenticity is the freedom to be as we are, the courage to live with integrity, the joy of embracing one's true nature. In authenticity, we find a happiness that is unwavering, a peace that is constant, a life that is full.

Imagine a flower blooming in the wild, free from constraint, open to the sun, unafraid of judgment. This is authenticity—a life lived in harmony with the self, a happiness that arises from self-acceptance, a joy that is as natural as the bloom. To be authentic is to live with a heart that is open, a spirit that is free, a soul that is unbound.

Authenticity is not about perfection; it is about wholeness, about embracing the light and the shadow, about honouring the flaws and the strengths. It is a way of being that allows us to experience happiness as a state of freedom, as a feeling of belonging, as a peace that arises from being true to oneself. For in authenticity, we find a life that is rich, a happiness that is full, a joy that is boundless.

Letting Go of Labels: Moving Beyond Societal Expectations

In our journey of self-understanding, we often encounter labels, expectations, and definitions imposed by society. We are told who we should be, what we should achieve, how we should live. These labels can be limiting, confining, stifling. To truly understand oneself, we must let go of these labels, we must free ourselves from societal expectations, we must allow ourselves to be as we are.

Letting go of labels is an act of liberation, a way of freeing the soul, a path to happiness that is unburdened, that is true, that is pure. When we release these expectations, we open ourselves to the fullness of our own being, we allow ourselves to discover our true values, our true passions, our true purpose.

Imagine breaking free from a cocoon, shedding the constraints, spreading one's wings, soaring into the open sky. This is the freedom of letting go—a happiness that arises from self-discovery, a joy that is rooted in authenticity, a peace that comes from living without constraint. For in letting go of labels, we find a life that is rich in possibility, a happiness that is boundless, a self that is true.

The Dynamic Self: Embracing Growth and Change

Identity is not a fixed concept; it is dynamic, evolving, ever-changing. To know oneself is to embrace this change, to see the self as a river that flows, a journey that unfolds, a story that is continually being written. Growth is a part of identity, a natural evolution, a process of becoming. The self is not a destination; it is a journey, a path, a dance of change.

Imagine a river that flows through mountains, valleys, forests, changing with each turn, with each season, with each moment. This is the self—a journey of growth, a process of transformation, a dance of becoming. To embrace the dynamic nature of the self is to find happiness in growth, to experience joy in evolution, to find peace in change.

To understand oneself is to accept that we are always becoming, that we are continually evolving, that we are free to grow, to change, to transform. It is to embrace a happiness that is rooted in growth, a joy that arises from self-discovery, a peace that is as constant as the journey itself. For in embracing the dynamic self, we find a life that is full, a happiness that is true, a self that is as vast as the soul.

Practices for Self-Understanding and Authentic Happiness

Self-understanding is a practice, a journey, a way of living that requires reflection, honesty, and love. Below are practices that can help us explore the self, that can guide us on the path to authenticity, that can cultivate a life that is rich in happiness, in peace, in fulfilment.

1. Engage in Journaling: Take time each day to write about your thoughts, your feelings, your dreams, your fears. This practice of journaling helps to create a sense of self-awareness, to foster introspection, to cultivate a life that is grounded in understanding, in authenticity, in joy.

2. Practice Mindful Reflection: Spend time in quiet reflection, exploring your beliefs, your values, your desires, your experiences. This practice of mindful reflection helps to bring clarity to the self, to foster a deeper connection with your own soul, to embrace a life that is rich in self-awareness.

3. Embrace Meditation and Inner Stillness: Use meditation as a way of connecting with your inner self, of

finding peace in the stillness, of exploring the depths of your being. This practice of meditation helps to create a sense of calm, to foster presence, to embrace a life that is rooted in inner peace.

4. Live Authentically and Honour Your Truths: Practice living in alignment with your values, your passions, your essence. This practice of authenticity helps to create a sense of freedom, to foster self-confidence, to cultivate a life that is true to your own soul, your own spirit, your own heart.

5. Celebrate Growth and Embrace Change: Honour the journey of the self, the process of becoming, the beauty of growth. This practice of celebrating growth helps to create a sense of joy, to inspire a spirit of self-acceptance, to foster a life that is rich in evolution, in transformation, in happiness.

The Joy of Self-Understanding: A Life That is True

Self-understanding is a pathway to happiness, a source of peace, a way of finding joy through authenticity, through acceptance, through love. It is a happiness that arises not from becoming someone else, but from becoming oneself, a joy that is rooted in self-discovery, a peace that is as steady as the soul, as vast as the heart, as true as the self.

As we continue this journey, may we carry with us the courage to explore the self, the wisdom to embrace our authenticity, the knowledge that we are enough, that we are complete, that we are beautiful as we are.

From the enigma of the self, we find a happiness that is deep, a joy that is steady, a peace that is as boundless as the love we hold within.

CHAPTER 28: RESILIENCE THROUGH ADVERSITY – FINDING STRENGTH IN SORROW

Life is a journey through seasons, an unfolding of joy and sorrow, of light and shadow, of triumph and trial. In times of sorrow, when the heart is heavy, when the path is dark, when hope seems distant, it is resilience that carries us through, that lifts us up, that guides us toward the dawn. Resilience is the strength that arises from within, a quiet courage, a gentle persistence, a light that endures even in the darkest of hours.

To experience hardship is to walk through fire, to face challenges that test the spirit, to encounter sorrows that shake the soul. But in these moments of adversity, we discover a strength we did not know we possessed, a resilience that arises not from avoiding sorrow, but from embracing it, from learning from it, from growing through it. Hardship is a profound teacher, a guide that deepens our understanding, that expands our hearts, that enriches our capacity for joy, for love, for life.

In this chapter, we explore the beauty of resilience, the strength that arises from sorrow, the joy that is born from enduring hardship. For in resilience, we find a happiness that is unshakable, a peace that is steadfast, a life that is rich in strength, in wisdom, in grace.

The Path through Sorrow: Embracing Hardship as a Teacher

Sorrow is a path that none of us wish to walk, but it is a path that we all, at some point, must travel. To face sorrow is to confront life's fragility, to encounter pain, to experience loss. Yet within this sorrow lies a hidden gift, a lesson, a wisdom that can only be found by journeying through the darkness. Hardship, when embraced, becomes a teacher, a guide that shows us the strength within, the courage we carry, the resilience we hold.

Imagine a tree standing in the midst of a storm, its branches bending, its leaves shaking, its roots holding steady. The storm does not break the tree; it strengthens it, it deepens its roots, it makes it resilient. Sorrow, too, is like this storm, a force that tests us, that bends us, that strengthens our roots. Through hardship, we find a resilience that is deep, a strength that is steady, a peace that arises from knowing we have endured, we have overcome, we have grown.

To embrace sorrow as a teacher is to find meaning in adversity, to seek wisdom in struggle, to recognize that even in our darkest hours, there is light, there is hope, there is a strength that carries us forward. For in sorrow, we find a depth that enriches our lives, a resilience that empowers us, a happiness that is rooted in understanding, in acceptance, in grace.

The Quiet Strength of Resilience: Enduring with Grace

Resilience is not a loud strength; it is a quiet, steady endurance, a gentle resolve, a strength that whispers, "I will carry on." It is the courage to rise after falling, the grace to continue despite the pain, the faith to believe that this, too, shall pass. Resilience is the strength that endures, the spirit that perseveres, the heart that holds steady in the face of sorrow.

Imagine a river flowing over rocks, around obstacles, carving its way through the landscape. The river does not force its way; it flows with grace, it moves with resilience, it finds a way. Resilience is like this river—a strength that adapts, that endures, that finds a path through the challenges, through the sorrows, through the darkness.

To cultivate resilience is to cultivate a heart that is open, a spirit that is flexible, a mind that is patient. It is to trust in our own ability to endure, to find peace in the process, to embrace the journey. For in resilience, we find a strength that is unwavering, a peace that is enduring, a life that is as resilient as the river, as steady as the heart, as boundless as the soul.

The Gift of Growth: Transforming Pain into Strength

Sorrow has the power to transform us, to deepen us, to grow us in ways that joy cannot. When we face hardship, we are given an opportunity to grow, to expand, to become. Pain is a catalyst, a force that shapes us, that refines us, that strengthens us. It is in facing our struggles that we discover our courage, that we cultivate resilience, that we find meaning in the midst of suffering.

Imagine a seed buried in the soil, enduring the weight, the darkness, the pressure. Yet from this pressure, the seed grows, it breaks through the soil, it reaches toward the light. Hardship, too, is like this soil, a weight that feels heavy, a darkness that seems endless, but it is also a source of growth, a path to transformation, a journey of becoming.

To embrace pain as a source of growth is to find joy in resilience, to experience peace in the process, to recognize the beauty in becoming. For in our struggles, we find a strength that is profound, a resilience that is true, a happiness that is as steady as the self that has endured, that has grown, that has risen.

The Depth of Empathy: Sorrow as a Path to Compassion

Hardship does not only strengthen us; it softens us, it deepens our empathy, it opens our hearts. When we face sorrow, we come to understand the struggles of others, we feel a compassion that is deep, a kindness that is boundless, a love that is as vast as the heart itself. Sorrow is a bridge to connection, a reminder of our shared humanity, a source of empathy, of compassion, of love.

Imagine a person who has known sorrow, who has felt pain, who has endured loss. This person carries within them a depth, a kindness, a warmth that comes from understanding, from experience, from compassion. Sorrow, when embraced, becomes a source of empathy, a pathway to connection, a way of understanding the heart of another.

To find strength in sorrow is to find love in resilience, to experience compassion in adversity, to recognize that our struggles connect us, unite us, bring us closer. For in sorrow, we find a love that is deep, a kindness that is pure, a life that is rich in empathy, in connection, in joy.

The Joy of Resilience: A Happiness Rooted in Strength

Resilience is a pathway to happiness, a source of joy, a strength that arises from enduring, from persevering, from growing. To be resilient is to experience a happiness that is not dependent on circumstance, a joy that arises not from avoiding sorrow, but from embracing it, from learning from it, from finding meaning in it. Resilience teaches us that we are capable, that we are strong, that we are unbreakable.

Imagine standing on a mountain after a long, difficult climb, feeling the strength in your legs, the pride in your heart, the joy in your soul. This is the joy of resilience— a happiness that arises from knowing we have overcome, we have grown, we have become. It is a happiness that is deep, a joy that is steady, a peace that is rooted in strength, in resilience, in grace.

To find joy in resilience is to find a life that is rich in meaning, a happiness that is unwavering, a peace that is as profound as the strength we carry within. For in resilience, we find a life that is full, a happiness that is true, a self that is as resilient as the soul.

Practices for Cultivating Resilience and Embracing Hardship as Growth

Resilience is a practice, a journey, a way of living that requires strength, patience, and love. Below are practices that can help us cultivate resilience, that can guide us on the path to strength, that can create a life that is rich in peace, in joy, in endurance.

1. Practice Self-Compassion: Treat yourself with kindness, with patience, with love in times of hardship. This practice of self-compassion helps to create a foundation of resilience, to foster inner peace, to embrace a life that is grounded in self-acceptance, in patience, in joy.

2. Reflect on Past Resilience: Take time to reflect on the challenges you have faced, the hardships you have endured, the strength you have discovered. This practice of reflection helps to create a sense of pride, to foster self-awareness, to cultivate a life that is rich in strength, in resilience, in peace.

3. Embrace Emotional Release: Allow yourself to feel, to express, to release your emotions. This practice of emotional release helps to create a sense of freedom, to foster resilience, to find peace in the act of letting go, of embracing the fullness of your own experience.

4. Seek Meaning in Hardship: Practice finding meaning in adversity, seeing challenges as opportunities for growth, recognizing sorrow as a teacher. This practice of seeking meaning helps to create a sense of purpose, to foster resilience, to embrace a life that is rich in depth, in

wisdom, in joy.

5. Cultivate Gratitude for Growth: Take time to appreciate the strength that has arisen from hardship, the resilience that has developed, the growth that has occurred. This practice of gratitude helps to create a sense of appreciation, to foster a spirit of resilience, to find joy in the journey of becoming.

The Strength of Resilience: A Life That is Whole

Resilience is a path to happiness, a source of peace, a way of finding strength through adversity, through sorrow, through growth. It is a happiness that arises not from escaping hardship, but from embracing it, a joy that is rooted in strength, a peace that is as steady as the heart, as vast as the soul, as true as the self.

As we continue this journey, may we carry with us the courage to endure, the wisdom to grow, the knowledge that we are capable, that we are resilient, that we are whole.

In resilience, we find a happiness that is deep, a joy that is steady, a peace that is as boundless as the love we hold within.

CHAPTER 29: LEGACY OF JOY – THE HAPPINESS WE LEAVE BEHIND

A life lived with joy is not only a gift to oneself; it is a gift to the world, a light that radiates beyond the boundaries of the self, a warmth that touches others, a legacy that lingers in hearts and minds long after we are gone. Happiness, when cultivated with purpose and kindness, becomes a ripple that spreads outward, a legacy that inspires, a memory that uplifts. To live with joy is to create a footprint of love, a pathway of light, a legacy of happiness.

We often think of legacy in terms of achievements, titles, or material wealth. But the true legacy of a life well-lived lies not in what we have accumulated, but in what we have given, not in what we have acquired, but in what we have shared. It is the kindness we show, the laughter we inspire, the compassion we extend that leaves a lasting imprint, a mark on the hearts of those who cross our path. The happiness we cultivate within ourselves becomes a beacon for others, a source of inspiration, a legacy of joy.

In this chapter, we explore the concept of leaving behind a legacy of joy, of living in a way that uplifts, that inspires, that transcends the self. For in creating a life rich in purpose, in kindness, in joy, we find a happiness that endures, a peace that is timeless, a legacy that lives on.

The Ripple Effect of Joy: How Happiness Inspires Others

Joy is a force that moves beyond the self, a light that spreads, a warmth that touches others. When we live with happiness, when we cultivate joy within, we inspire others to do the same. A smile shared, a kindness extended, a compassion offered—all of these acts create ripples of happiness that reach beyond us, that influence others, that contribute to a legacy of joy.

Imagine the ripple created by a single drop in a still pond, each wave reaching further, touching the shore, expanding outward. This is the effect of happiness—a legacy that spreads, a joy that multiplies, a kindness that echoes. To live with joy is to create this ripple, to touch the lives of others, to inspire happiness that reaches beyond oneself.

To leave behind a legacy of joy is to live with awareness, to recognize that our happiness impacts others, that our kindness inspires, that our actions create waves of joy that touch lives in ways we may never know. For in the ripple effect of joy, we find a legacy that is enduring, a happiness that is expansive, a life that is rich in love, in kindness, in connection.

Purpose as the Heart of a Joyful Legacy: Living with Intention

A life lived with purpose is a life that leaves a lasting impact, a legacy that speaks to the heart, a happiness that is rooted in meaning. Purpose is the core of a joyful legacy, the reason that drives us, the passion that fuels us, the cause that calls us. To live with purpose is to align our actions with our values, to contribute to something greater, to create a life that is rich in meaning, in fulfilment, in joy.

Imagine a candle that burns with a steady flame, its light illuminating the darkness, its warmth spreading comfort, its presence bringing peace. This is a life lived with purpose—a legacy that shines, a joy that endures, a happiness that is shared. Purpose is the light that guides us, the force that inspires us, the heart of a legacy that lives on.

To create a legacy of joy, we must live with purpose, with intention, with clarity. We must align our actions with our values, our lives with our dreams, our hearts with our passions. For in living with purpose, we create a legacy that is rich in meaning, a happiness that is deep, a life that is fulfilled.

Kindness as the Foundation of a Lasting Happiness

Kindness is the language of love, a gesture that bridges hearts, a force that transcends boundaries. A legacy built on kindness is a legacy that endures, a happiness that resonates, a joy that lives on. To be kind is to offer a part of ourselves, to extend a hand, to share in the joys and sorrows of others. Kindness is not only an act; it is a way of being, a way of living, a way of creating a legacy that is as gentle as it is profound.

Imagine a garden tended with care, each flower blooming, each leaf growing, each stem reaching toward the sun. Kindness is like this garden—a legacy that grows, a joy that flourishes, a happiness that is shared. When we live with kindness, we plant seeds of happiness, we create a legacy that nourishes, that uplifts, that endures.

To create a legacy of joy is to live with a heart that is open, to offer kindness without expectation, to share happiness without restraint. For in kindness, we find a happiness that is timeless, a peace that is enduring, a life that is as rich as the love we give, as fulfilling as the joy we share, as beautiful as the legacy we leave behind.

The Joy of Giving: Creating a Legacy of Generosity

To give is to create a happiness that is not confined by the self, a joy that reaches beyond, a legacy that lives on. Giving is a way of sharing our joy, of spreading our happiness, of creating a life that is rich in generosity, in compassion, in love. When we give, we contribute to the happiness of others, we create a ripple of joy, we build a legacy that is generous, that is fulfilling, that is true.

Imagine a river that flows freely, its waters nourishing the earth, its presence sustaining life, its flow creating beauty. This is the joy of giving—a happiness that is shared, a legacy that is generous, a life that is abundant. To give is to live with an open heart, to share with an open hand, to create a legacy that is as expansive as the river, as nourishing as the earth, as boundless as love.

To create a legacy of joy, we must give freely, generously, compassionately. We must offer our time, our presence, our kindness. For in giving, we find a happiness that is rich, a peace that is deep, a life that is as fulfilling as the love we give, as abundant as the joy we share.

Living for Others: Finding Fulfilment in Connection

A life lived for others is a life that is rich in connection, a happiness that is shared, a legacy that is profound. When we live for others, we find fulfilment in connection, we experience joy in community, we create a legacy that is rooted in love, in empathy, in understanding. To live for others is to recognize that happiness is not solitary, that joy is not isolated, that fulfilment is found in the bonds we create, the lives we touch, the love we share.

Imagine a circle of friends, each one supporting the other, each one contributing to the joy, the peace, the love. This is the power of connection—a happiness that is shared, a legacy that is collective, a life that is enriched by the presence of others. To live for others is to live with a heart that is open, a spirit that is generous, a soul that is connected.

To create a legacy of joy, we must live with love, with empathy, with connection. We must recognize the beauty of unity, the power of community, the joy of belonging. For in living for others, we find a happiness that is boundless, a peace that is profound, a life that is rich in love, in friendship, in connection.

Practices for Cultivating a Legacy of Joy and Creating Lasting Happiness

Leaving a legacy of joy is a practice, a journey, a way of living that requires love, intention, and kindness. Below are practices that can help us create a legacy of joy, that can guide us on the path to purpose, that can cultivate a life that is rich in connection, in generosity, in happiness.

1. Live with Purpose and Intention: Align your actions with your values, live with clarity, pursue what brings meaning. This practice of purposeful living helps to create a life that is rich in fulfilment, that contributes to a legacy of joy, that fosters lasting happiness.

2. Extend Kindness and Compassion: Show kindness to others, extend compassion, offer empathy. This practice of kindness helps to create a life that is rich in love, that builds a legacy of happiness, that inspires others.

3. Give Generously and Freely: Share your time, your resources, your love. This practice of giving helps to create a life that is rich in generosity, that fosters a legacy of joy, that spreads happiness.

4. Nurture Connections and Community: Build meaningful relationships, foster a sense of community, live with a heart that is open to others. This practice of connection helps to create a life that is rich in friendship, that contributes to a legacy of joy, that cultivates happiness.

5. Reflect on Your Impact and Legacy: Take time to reflect on the legacy you are creating, the happiness you are sharing, the lives you are touching. This practice of reflection helps to create a life that is intentional, that fosters a legacy of joy, that inspires others.

The Legacy of Joy: A Life That is Lasting

A legacy of joy is a pathway to happiness, a source of inspiration, a life that is as enduring as the love we share, as lasting as the kindness we give, as profound as the happiness we cultivate. It is a happiness that is not bound by time, a joy that reaches beyond the self, a legacy that lives on in the hearts of others.

As we continue this journey, may we carry with us the knowledge that our joy creates ripples, that our kindness builds a legacy, that our lives are enriched by the love we give, the connections we make, the happiness we leave behind.

For in creating a legacy of joy, we find a happiness that is timeless, a peace that is profound, a life that is as boundless as the love we hold within.

CHAPTER 30: THE EVERLASTING PURSUIT OF JOY

Happiness is not a destination; it is a journey, a path that winds and weaves through the tapestry of our lives, a quest as eternal as the stars, as infinite as the ocean. To pursue happiness is to embark on an odyssey of the heart, a voyage of the soul, a timeless dance with beauty, with love, with wonder. The pursuit of joy is the art of embracing each moment as it comes, of finding grace in the ebb and flow, of surrendering to the rhythm of existence with a heart that is open, a spirit that is free, a soul that is vast.

As we stand at the threshold of this journey, gazing back upon the paths we have traversed—the lessons learned, the wisdom gleaned, the joy uncovered—we recognize that happiness is not something we acquire; it is something we cultivate, something we become, something we awaken to with each breath, each step, each heartbeat. The pursuit of happiness is not an end; it is an endless unfolding, a perpetual becoming, a ceaseless return to the beauty of the present, the wonder of the now, the miracle of being alive.

In this final chapter, we reflect on the everlasting pursuit of joy, on the ways in which this journey transforms us, uplifts us, deepens us. For to seek happiness is to live with wonder, to walk with gratitude, to love with abandon. It is a journey without conclusion, an adventure without boundaries, a pursuit that is as boundless as the soul, as timeless as the stars, as eternal as the dance of life itself.

Gratitude as the Guiding Light of the Journey

Gratitude is the light that illuminates the path, the gentle flame that guides us, the compass that points us to the beauty of the present. To live with gratitude is to see each moment as a gift, each breath as a blessing, each heartbeat as a miracle. Gratitude transforms our pursuit of happiness into a journey of appreciation, a pilgrimage of wonder, a dance of joy. It is the practice of noticing, of cherishing, of honouring the simple, the ordinary, the fleeting.

Imagine walking through a field of wildflowers, each one unique, each one beautiful, each one fleeting. Gratitude is like this field—a reminder of the abundance around us, the beauty within us, the joy that is always present, always available, always here. To live with gratitude is to walk this field with open eyes, with a heart that sees, with a soul that feels.

To carry gratitude with us on this journey is to find happiness not only in the extraordinary, but in the everyday, not only in the destination, but in each step, each breath, each moment. For in gratitude, we find a happiness that is grounded, a joy that is enduring, a peace that is as steady as the rhythm of life itself.

The Wonder of Life: Embracing the Mystery and the Marvel

Life is a mystery, a marvel, a cosmic dance of beauty and change, of joy and sorrow, of light and shadow. To pursue happiness is to embrace this mystery, to live with wonder, to approach each moment with a heart that is curious, a spirit that is adventurous, a soul that is open to the unknown. Wonder is the essence of joy, the foundation of awe, the breath that connects us to the infinite, to the eternal, to the divine.

Imagine standing beneath a night sky, the stars stretching endlessly, the universe vast, the silence profound. In this moment of wonder, there is no need for answers, no search for certainty, no desire for control. There is only presence, only peace, only the joy of being. Wonder is like this night sky—a vastness that invites us to let go, to surrender, to be.

To live with wonder is to embrace the enigma of existence, to find beauty in the questions, to experience joy in the mystery. It is to walk the path of happiness with a heart that is open to surprise, a mind that is free from expectation, a soul that is at peace with the unknown. For in wonder, we find a happiness that is boundless, a joy that is infinite, a life that is as expansive as the universe, as luminous as the stars, as endless as the journey itself.

The Power of Love: The Heart of Joy's Journey

Love is the heart of the pursuit of joy, the essence of happiness, the force that binds us, connects us, transforms us. To love is to open ourselves to vulnerability, to joy, to sorrow, to connection. It is to experience life with a heart that is tender, a spirit that is giving, a soul that is generous. Love is the light that illuminates the path, the warmth that sustains us, the joy that multiplies as it is shared, as it is given, as it is received.

Imagine a candle that burns with a steady flame, its warmth spreading, its light touching, its presence bringing peace. Love is like this candle—a legacy that endures, a joy that expands, a happiness that is rooted in giving, in sharing, in connecting. To live with love is to experience a happiness that is not confined to the self, but that reaches beyond, that touches others, that creates a legacy of joy.

To pursue happiness with love is to create a life that is rich in connection, a heart that is full of kindness, a spirit that is abundant in generosity. For in love, we find a happiness that is enduring, a joy that is fulfilling, a life that is as rich as the love we give, as beautiful as the love we share, as profound as the love we are.

Embracing the Journey: Living with Openness, Courage, and Wonder

The pursuit of happiness is a journey that invites us to live with openness, to walk with courage, to embrace life with wonder. It is a path that calls us to be present, to be aware, to be alive. To pursue happiness is to live with a heart that is open to experience, a mind that is curious, a soul that is ready to receive the beauty, the mystery, the joy of existence.

Imagine a path that winds through fields and forests, over mountains and rivers, beneath skies that change with the seasons, with the hours, with the light. This is the journey of happiness—a path that is ever-changing, ever-beautiful, ever-new. It is a journey that has no end, a pursuit that is boundless, a quest that is timeless.

To embrace this journey is to live with a spirit that is adventurous, to seek happiness not as a final destination, but as an ever-present companion, a source of joy, a way of being. For in embracing the journey, we find a happiness that is as endless as the path itself, a joy that is as constant as the heart, a peace that is as vast as the soul.

The Everlasting Pursuit: A Life That is Full of Joy, Wonder, and Love

Happiness is a pursuit that has no end, a journey that is as infinite as life, as timeless as love, as eternal as the soul. To seek happiness is to live with gratitude, to walk with wonder, to love with abandon. It is to embrace each moment as it comes, to find beauty in the fleeting, to experience joy in the becoming. The pursuit of happiness is not about reaching a destination; it is about creating a life that is full, a heart that is open, a soul that is at peace.

Imagine a circle, infinite and unbroken, a journey that continues, a path that unfolds, a dance that never ends. This is the pursuit of joy—a life that is rich in gratitude, a happiness that is grounded in wonder, a peace that is rooted in love. It is a journey that we take not once, but forever, a quest that calls us to be fully alive, to be fully present, to be fully ourselves.

As we continue this journey, may we carry with us the wisdom of the path, the light of gratitude, the beauty of wonder, the power of love. May we remember that happiness is not a place, but a way of being, not an end, but a beginning, not a possession, but a presence. For in the everlasting pursuit of joy, we find a life that is full, a heart that is open, a soul that is free.

May our journey be one of gratitude, one of love, one of wonder. And may we find, in the pursuit of happiness, a life that is boundless, a joy that is timeless, a peace that is as vast as the love we hold within.

EPILOGUE – A JOURNEY THAT LIVES ON

As this journey comes to its written end, let us pause, take a deep breath, and hold this moment close. We have traversed landscapes vast and varied, exploring what it means to live with joy, purpose, resilience, and wonder. Together, we have sought happiness not as a fleeting feeling, but as an essence, a way of being that infuses each moment, each thought, each breath.

This journey toward happiness is as timeless as the tides, as enduring as the mountains, as profound as the stars that glow in the boundless night. To seek happiness is not to grasp at a single moment of bliss, but to open ourselves to the fullness of life, to welcome the beauty and the challenge, the joy and the sorrow, the light and the shadow. For it is in this completeness, in this paradox, that we find a happiness that is true, that is lasting, that is whole.

If there is one wisdom to take forward, let it be that happiness is an unfolding—a journey that begins anew with each sunrise, each heartbeat, each decision to live fully, to love deeply, to give freely. Happiness, we have learned, is not a destination on some distant horizon, but a companion on the path, a presence that we invite into our lives through our thoughts, our actions, our way of being. It is found not in perfection, but in authenticity; not in certainty, but in openness; not in arrival, but in the journey itself.

The Art of Gratitude: A Path Back to the Heart

Gratitude, as we have come to understand, is the gateway to a life rich in meaning and joy. To live with gratitude is to cultivate a heart that recognizes the extraordinary in the ordinary, that sees beauty in the simple, that finds abundance in what is already here. Gratitude is not merely an expression; it is a way of seeing, a way of loving, a way of being. When we live with gratitude, we awaken to the gifts that surround us, the blessings that sustain us, the moments that bring us back to the heart.

Imagine carrying this gratitude with you, like a gentle flame, illuminating even the darkest corners of life. Imagine this gratitude as a lens through which you see the world, a bridge that connects you to others, a force that deepens your connection to life itself. For in gratitude, we find the essence of happiness—a contentment that is not dependent on what we have, but on who we are, a peace that is not given, but chosen, a joy that is as steady as the breath.

The Wonder of Being Alive: Embracing Life's Endless Mystery

As we walk this path of happiness, let us also embrace the wonder of existence—the mystery, the beauty, the unknown. Wonder is the soul's recognition of life's boundless beauty, an acknowledgment of the magic that lives within the ordinary, the sublime that hides within the simple. To live with wonder is to approach life with a childlike heart, a mind open to mystery, a spirit ready to be amazed. Wonder transforms the everyday into the extraordinary, the routine into the remarkable, the fleeting into the unforgettable.

Imagine looking at the world with eyes wide open, with a heart that is curious, with a soul that is in awe. Imagine finding wonder in a quiet moment, in a familiar smile, in the rustling of leaves, in the laughter of friends. Wonder is not something we find; it is something we bring to each moment, each encounter, each day. To live with wonder is to see life as an unfolding gift, to approach each day as an invitation, to recognize that happiness is not something we search for, but something we allow ourselves to experience, to embrace, to become.

Living with Love: The Heart of Happiness

At the heart of happiness lies love—the love we extend to others, the kindness we show to strangers, the compassion we offer to ourselves. Love is the foundation of a joyful life, the thread that binds us, the light that heals us, the warmth that sustains us. To love is to live with an open heart, to see the beauty in others, to recognize our shared humanity, to find joy in connection. Love is the happiness that grows as it is given, the peace that deepens as it is shared, the grace that expands as it is expressed.

Imagine carrying this love with you, like a song that never fades, a warmth that never diminishes, a joy that only grows. Imagine loving not just those who are dear to you, but the world around you, the life within you, the journey before you. Love, when embraced fully, becomes the foundation of happiness, the core of joy, the essence of peace. To live with love is to live a life that is full, a life that is rich, a life that is as deep as the heart itself.

The Courage to Continue: Embracing Happiness as a Lifelong Journey

As we reach the final pages, let us remember that happiness is not a single destination, a final achievement, a perfect state. It is a path that we walk, a choice that we make, a way of being that we cultivate. Happiness is a journey that continues as long as we breathe, as long as we live, as long as we seek.

To pursue happiness is to live with courage, to face life with an open heart, to embrace each moment with grace. It is to walk this path knowing that there will be challenges, knowing that there will be sorrow, knowing that there will be days of struggle. But it is also to know that there will be beauty, that there will be love, that there will be joy beyond measure.

So, as you step forward, may you carry with you the wisdom of this journey—the gratitude, the wonder, the love, the courage. May you continue to seek happiness with a heart that is open, a mind that is curious, a soul that is ready to embrace life in all its fullness. And may you find, in each day, a reason to smile, a moment to cherish, a life to live.

Happiness is the Journey of Becoming

Happiness is not something we find; it is something we become. It is not a prize to be won, but a presence to be felt. It is the gentle unfolding of the heart, the quiet expansion of the soul, the deepening of love, of gratitude, of wonder. Happiness is the gift we give to ourselves, the joy we offer to others, the legacy we leave behind.

As this journey of words comes to its end, may the journey of your happiness continue. May you find in these pages not only inspiration, but companionship; not only lessons, but reminders; not only words, but wisdom. And may you walk forward with a heart that is full, a spirit that is alive, a soul that is at peace.

Through the everlasting pursuit of joy, we find a life that is rich, a love that is boundless, a happiness that is as endless as the journey itself.

With deepest gratitude and boundless hope,

Dr Bhaskar Bora

REFERENCES

1. Fredrickson, B. L. (2001). The role of positive emotions in positive psychology: The broaden-and-build theory of positive emotions. American Psychologist, 56(3), 218-226.

2. Csikszentmihalyi, M. (1990). Flow: The psychology of optimal experience. Harper & Row.

3. Seligman, M. E. P. (2002). Authentic Happiness: Using the New Positive Psychology to Realize Your Potential for Lasting Fulfilment. Free Press.

4. Lyubomirsky, S., Sheldon, K. M., & Schkade, D. (2005). Pursuing happiness: The architecture of sustainable change. Review of General Psychology, 9(2), 111-131.

5. Peterson, C., & Seligman, M. E. P. (2004). Character Strengths and Virtues: A Handbook and Classification. Oxford University Press.

6. Brown, B. (2012). Daring Greatly: How the Courage to Be Vulnerable Transforms the Way We Live, Love, Parent, and Lead. Gotham Books.

7. Emmons, R. A., & McCullough, M. E. (2003). Counting blessings versus burdens: An experimental investigation of gratitude and subjective well-being in daily life. Journal of Personality and Social Psychology, 84(2),

377-389.

8. Kabat-Zinn, J. (1994). Wherever You Go, There You Are: Mindfulness Meditation in Everyday Life. Hyperion.

9. Neff, K. D. (2003). Self-compassion: An alternative conceptualization of a healthy attitude toward oneself. Self and Identity, 2(2), 85-101.

10. Dweck, C. S. (2006). Mindset: The New Psychology of Success. Random House.

11. Ryff, C. D., & Keyes, C. L. M. (1995). The structure of psychological well-being revisited. Journal of Personality and Social Psychology, 69(4), 719-727.

12. Deci, E. L., & Ryan, R. M. (2000). The "what" and "why" of goal pursuits: Human needs and the self-determination of behavior. Psychological Inquiry, 11(4), 227-268.

13. Siegel, D. J. (2010). The Mindful Therapist: A Clinician's Guide to Mindsight and Neural Integration. W.W. Norton & Company.

14. Brach, T. (2003). Radical Acceptance: Embracing Your Life with the Heart of a Buddha. Bantam.

15. Frankl, V. E. (1984). Man's Search for Meaning. Washington Square Press.

16. Graham, S. (2009). Gratitude and well-being: A review and theoretical integration. Clinical Psychology Review, 30(3), 304-310.

17. Keltner, D., & Haidt, J. (2003). Approaching awe, a moral, spiritual, and aesthetic emotion. Cognition and Emotion, 17(2), 297-314.

18. Haidt, J. (2006). The Happiness Hypothesis: Finding Modern Truth in Ancient Wisdom. Basic Books.

19. Rogers, C. R. (1961). On Becoming a Person: A Therapist's View of Psychotherapy. Houghton Mifflin.

20. Kashdan, T. B., & Rottenberg, J. (2010). Psychological flexibility as a fundamental aspect of health. Clinical Psychology Review, 30(7), 865-878.

21. Baumeister, R. F., & Leary, M. R. (1995). The need to belong: Desire for interpersonal attachments as a fundamental human motivation. Psychological Bulletin, 117(3), 497-529.

22. Watkins, P. C., Woodward, K., Stone, T., & Kolts, R. L. (2003). Gratitude and happiness: Development of a measure of gratitude, and relationships with subjective well-being. Social Behavior and Personality, 31(5), 431-451.

23. Davidson, R. J., & McEwen, B. S. (2012). Social influences on neuroplasticity: Stress and interventions to promote well-being. Nature Neuroscience, 15(5), 689-695.

24. Gilbert, P. (2009). The Compassionate Mind: A New Approach to Life's Challenges. New Harbinger Publications.

25. Hanh, T. N. (2011). Peace Is Every Step: The Path of Mindfulness in Everyday Life. Bantam.

26. Lopez, S. J., & Snyder, C. R. (Eds.). (2011). The Oxford Handbook of Positive Psychology. Oxford University Press.

27. Shapiro, S. L., Carlson, L. E., Astin, J. A., & Freedman, B. (2006). Mechanisms of mindfulness. Journal of Clinical Psychology, 62(3), 373-386.

28. Snyder, C. R., & Lopez, S. J. (2007). Positive Psychology: The Scientific and Practical Explorations of Human Strengths. SAGE Publications.

29. Maslow, A. H. (1943). A theory of human motivation. Psychological Review, 50(4), 370-396.

30. Niemiec, R. M. (2018). Character Strengths Interventions: A Field Guide for Practitioners. Hogrefe Publishing.

ACKNOWLEDGEME NTS

Creating this book has been a journey of exploration, reflection, and collaboration, and I am deeply grateful to everyone who contributed their wisdom, support, and encouragement along the way.

First and foremost, I extend my heartfelt gratitude to my family and friends for their unwavering support and patience throughout this project. Your kindness, understanding, and belief in me provided the foundation upon which this work was built.

I am indebted to the many pioneers in the field of positive psychology whose research and insights inspired much of the material in this book. Their contributions have shaped the field, and their dedication to understanding happiness, resilience, and well-being has made a significant impact on our lives.

Thank you to my editor and the team at Irene Minds for their guidance and invaluable feedback, which helped shape this book into its final form. Your expertise, creativity, and attention to detail brought this project to life in ways I could not have achieved alone.

Finally, to the readers: this book was written for you.

May it serve as a source of inspiration, guidance, and encouragement as you journey toward a life rich in happiness, purpose, and peace. Thank you for embarking on this path with me.

With gratitude,
Dr Bhaskar Bora

COPYRIGHT INFORMATION

Title: The Science of Happiness: Lessons from Positive Psychology
Author: Dr Bhaskar Bora
Publisher: Irene Minds
Year of Publication: 2024
Contact Information: bora.dr@gmail.com

DISCLAIMER

The material contained in this book is provided for educational and informational purposes only. While every effort has been made to ensure that the content is accurate and complete, the author and publisher assume no responsibility for errors, inaccuracies, or omissions. The information and advice provided in this book do not constitute medical, psychological, or professional advice, and should not be relied upon as such.

The reader is encouraged to consult with a qualified professional before making any decisions or undertaking any practices discussed in this book. The author and publisher disclaim any liability for any damages, personal or otherwise, resulting from the use of the information contained in this book.

This book is not intended to replace the guidance of a licensed therapist, psychologist, or medical professional. The experiences and insights shared are based on positive psychology principles and research, and are offered as general guidance for those interested in personal development, well-being, and happiness.

www.ingramcontent.com/pod-product-compliance
Lightning Source LLC
Chambersburg PA
CBHW051555250726
48653CB00004BA/1165